MARK. PLAN. TEACH.

Praise for *MARK. PLAN. TEACH.*

'Teachers go beyond the call of duty for our children. However, this book enables them to do even more in less time, which can support teachers in making a greater impact in the classroom. This is a must-read for all those who really want to tackle teacher workload to adopt classroom strategies that are easy to use, as well as grounded in research.'
Suella Fernandes, MP for Fareham and Chair of Governors, Michaela Community School

'Marking can have a massive impact on teacher workload. Worryingly, it often has very little impact on students' learning. Ross makes an important contribution by reminding us that marking is merely a type of feedback – and that there are other forms of feedback, verbal and in-lesson, for example. He emphasises that it is the quality, not the quantity, of marking and feedback that is important. Applied with care, these ideas can help build schools that work for pupils and for staff.'
Russell Hobby, General Secretary, NAHT 2010-2017

'There is a reason why Ross is the most followed British teacher on Twitter. He isn't didactic or patronising. He doesn't have a political agenda. He just wants to help educational professionals to be the very best they can be, using a combination of his personal experience and the wealth of expert voices at his disposal.'
Natasha Devon MBE, Writer, Campaigner and Co-Founder of Self-Esteem Team

'What makes Ross special and this book crucial is the authentic, practical and accessible way the importance of feedback is addressed. Students deserve quality and teachers deserve support; this delivers on both, brilliantly!'
Richard Gerver, World Renowned Speaker and Author

'*Mark. Plan. Teach.* is soundly based on a mix of astute classroom understanding, sound leadership experience and relevant evidence. It is an absorbing read and will appeal to classroom practitioners, middle leaders and senior leaders alike.'
Kcarrie Valentine, Head of Professional Development Services, Association of School and College Leaders

'*Mark. Plan. Teach.* is packed with ideas that are simple to implement but will prove transformative to both teachers and learners. With a clear focus on proven, practical strategies and the psychology underpinning them, this is a book that will give teachers both the tools and the confidence they need to further their practice, save themselves time and improve learner outcomes.'
Dr Pooky Knightsmith, Director, Children, Young People and Schools Programme, Charlie Waller Memorial Trust

'Ross has been at the forefront of supporting teachers new to the profession. With this latest offering, he continues to clarify the essentials of excellence in the profession. It's a great mix of theory, current debate and practical advice for teachers new or seasoned.'
Bennie Kara, Deputy Headteacher

Bloomsbury Education
An imprint of Bloomsbury Publishing Plc

50 Bedford Square
London
WC1B 3DP
UK

1385 Broadway
New York
NY 10018
USA

www.bloomsbury.com

Bloomsbury is a registered trade mark of Bloomsbury Publishing Plc

First published 2017

A catalogue record for this book is available from the British Library.

ISBN:
PB: 9781472910875
ePub: 9781472910899
ePDF: 9781472910882

6 8 10 9 7 5

Design by Marcus Duck Design

Printed and bound by CPI Group (UK) Ltd, Croydon, CR0 4YY

This book is produced using paper that is made from wood grown in managed, sustainable forests. It is natural, renewable and recyclable. The logging and manufacturing processes conform to the environmental regulations of the country of origin.

To find out more about our authors and books visit www.bloomsbury.com. Here you will find extracts, author interviews, details of forthcoming events and the option to sign up for our newsletters.

MARK. PLAN. TEACH.

Save time. Reduce workload. Impact learning.

Ross Morrison McGill

B L O O M S B U R Y

LONDON · OXFORD · NEW YORK · NEW DELHI · SYDNEY

Other titles by Ross Morrison McGill

100 IDEAS FOR SECONDARY TEACHERS: OUTSTANDING LESSONS

A bank of inspirational ideas for managing behaviour, lesson planning, homework, assessment and all-round brilliant teaching, this book will change the way teachers think about their lessons. The ideas can be picked up five minutes before students arrive in class and put into practice just as they are, or embedded into day-to-day teaching to make every lesson consistently good.

TEACHER TOOLKIT

Packed with countless anecdotes from disastrous observations to marking in the broom cupboard, *TEACHER TOOLKIT* is a compendium of teaching strategies and advice, which aims to motivate, comfort, amuse and above all reduce the workload of any new teacher and help them survive their first five years in the job.

About the author

ROSS MORRISON McGILL is @TeacherToolkit, the most followed educator on Twitter in the UK and founder of one of the most popular education websites in the UK. He is an award-winning blogger, author and teacher with over twenty years of teaching and school leadership experience in some of the most challenging schools in London. In December 2015, he was nominated for The Sunday Times '500 Most Influential People in Britain' and remains the only classroom teacher to have featured to this day.

This book is for all those teachers who have had their careers blighted by school inspections.

Contents

. . . .

Section 1: Mark   **1**

Section 2: Plan   57

Section 3: Teach 115

And finally 170
Bibliography 176
Index 181

Acknowledgements

Firstly, to headteacher Alex Atherton, who supported the concept of **Mark. Plan. Teach.** and championed me to scribe the details of 'what all teachers should aspire to be and do' from classroom to classroom. The beginning of the process involved discussions, meetings, training sessions with colleagues, reading over twenty books and numerous journals, writing and tweaking content, and publishing excerpts online to gauge feedback. Over a period of 18 months, this evolved into a school policy that would offer consistency and clarity for teachers. The foundations of the work can be found throughout this book. So, I would like to thank Alex for sowing the seed for **Mark. Plan. Teach.** and for his initial contributions, which are threaded throughout these pages.

Whenever you find yourself reading this book, think about two things: one, if the content of what is written here is what *you* would like to champion as a teacher, how do you then consider this for a whole school? How do you create a teaching and learning culture where teachers have clarity, yet keep some autonomy in order to take risks? In a high-stakes economy, this is a difficult ask for all schools.

Secondly, teaching and learning policies, although useful, are not a statutory requirement for schools in England (Department for Education, 2014a). I suspect this is the same for the rest of the world (someone please tell me if not). The dilemma school leaders therefore face is this: if you wish to publish a teaching and learning policy to communicate consistency and clarity for your teaching staff, this is a large, ongoing and long-term task to unpick. Consultation, communication and collaboration are key, as well as regular updates and inductions for new staff. In many ways, working (and teaching) to the standards set by yourself to ensure 'collective teacher efficacy' (see Section 3, Idea 3, p. 128) is a wonderful thing to aspire to, but remember this: if you publish anything that is non-statutory, external agencies may just visit your school, test it and beat you over the head with it, because what is written and evaluated is not what is evident in your classrooms. Then, your work is undone and you may wish you hadn't bothered in the first place!

Having reflected on this over the past eight months whilst writing this book, I have since reshaped a twenty-page teaching and learning policy, which I'm confident no teacher has (ever) read from cover to cover in one sitting, into 'probably the best teaching and learning policy in the world'. A policy that would make expectations simpler, yet require any external pair of eyes to work harder for their time spent evaluating others in the classroom. If you are short on time (or patience), flick over to Section 3, Idea 4, p. 131 to find out how I've simplified what every teacher should do in every school into just three sentences. It is the perfect set of expectations for all teachers. It's clear, effective and communicates high expectations for every classroom teacher. Whether you wish to enforce this upon all teachers in your school to achieve collective efficacy or risk being bashed over the head by external agencies is your prerogative. Disclaimer: I would now advocate that all schools question the content of their teaching and learning policies.

Further acknowledgements

To former commissioning editor, **Miriam Davey**, who is flourishing in her new publishing role with the Chartered College of Teaching. You encouraged me through the initial phases of *Mark. Plan. Teach.*, particularly during a difficult time in my career when I was questioning my direction and purpose. Your calm and wry humour ensured I kept my head above the parapet.

Next, to **Hannah Marston** who took on the role of editing this beast of a manuscript – for her cool exterior when dealing with my workload tantrums and constant refusal to manage editorial deadlines. Hannah, thank you for your patience, understanding and for the chocolate brownies to help push me over the line.

Also, to the hundreds of educators who have inspired my thoughts across the years. To the hundreds of colleagues who have attended the professional development events I have organised. To the colleagues who have sent me countless messages via email and social media. Your contributions have fuelled my thinking and I thank you for that. More recently, to **Professor Dame Alison Peacock** for taking up the mantle of CEO at the Chartered College of Teaching to bring common sense and evidence-informed research work into every teacher's classroom, and for writing the foreword to this book. To **Dr Tim O'Brien** whose expertise and valuable contributions throughout *Mark. Plan. Teach.* have advanced what was an 'ideas book' to another dimension – one that can provide explanations for why we, as teachers and as students, do the things we do. To **Polly Nor** for her brilliant illustrations, which you will enjoy on many pages in this book. And to **Marcus Duck** for another truly fantastic text design.

Thank you to all the authors, educators, researchers and teachers who have inspired me throughout the writing of *Mark. Plan. Teach.* – you can find them all listed individually in the bibliography (p. 176). To Amjad Ali, Debra Kidd, Isabella Wallace, Kcarrie Valentine, Mark Anderson, Mary Myatt, Pam Fearnley and Richard Gerver, who have each supported me to change the way I look at things in my next chapter in education. To all those teachers who write on the TeacherToolkit website, whose thoughts have equally inspired this book, and to Dr Helen Woodley for her selfless help with proofreading *Mark. Plan. Teach.* in the final days before publication – thank you, Helen.

Finally, to Jenni and Freddie for giving me the space to write, inspiring me to be courageous and for reminding me every day that to remain balanced and healthy, you must keep moving – and be able to switch off.

Foreword

Mark. Plan. Teach. is packed full of ideas for busy teachers, offering strategies for effective assessment, planning and teaching. Ross Morrison McGill draws upon his extensive experience working in secondary schools to provide punchy practical advice. This is very helpful and ensures that the reader is grabbed by immediate, simple and powerful ideas.

Building on the extensive range of classroom resources provided by his extremely popular blog, Ross has organised the book into three fundamental areas:

1. Assess what has been learnt.

2. Plan in response to assessment.

3. Teach what is needed next.

He begins with the daily assessment process of marking and feedback, providing simple techniques for ensuring that both teacher and pupil know what has been learnt. He is keen to show that this does not need to be an arduous process of written marking and offers a range of methods for both teacher and student to gain clarity over what has been understood. He then illustrates how to ensure that student misconceptions uncovered during marking are addressed within planning. Planning with simple effectiveness aims for impact when it comes to the all-important final stage of the cycle: teaching. It is refreshing for assessment to be recognised as a fundamentally informative process rather than as an adjunct for accountability purposes.

In my role as CEO of the new Chartered College of Teaching, I am particularly pleased to provide the foreword for this book because this text embodies a much-needed future dialogue between the gritty reality of classrooms and theoretical research. In each section, Ross ensures that he highlights the available evidence that underpins his recommended stance or approach. Really powerfully, he also has the humility to request informed theoretical commentary from the perspective of educational psychology. Dr Tim O'Brien, Visiting Fellow in Psychology and Human Development at UCL Institute of Education, provides a fascinating psychological perspective on the key recommendations.

This combination of practicality, reference to research evidence and rigorous academic commentary forms a useful model for our profession. It is the ambition of the Chartered College of Teaching to enable teachers to clearly articulate why they have planned to teach in a particular way and how they know this is likely to have the greatest impact on learning. Importantly, Ross states several times that 'context is king'. This is at the heart of professionalism. It is never enough to take an idea or strategy in isolation and implement it without adaptation to the needs of the students.

I recommend this resource to you and hope that it will provide a starting point for dialogue, debate and further enrichment within schools and via social media. Dialogue amongst informed teachers can form a vital part of professional learning. I hope you enjoy the prompts, nudges and challenges offered here and feel inspired to try new things out in the classroom and contribute to the furthering of professional knowledge that is so needed.

Professor Dame Alison Peacock
Chief Executive, Chartered College of Teaching

Introduction

In a landscape fuelled increasingly by data and lack of funding, teachers' workload is at its highest level. With mounting concerns and growing evidence to suggest that teacher recruitment, retention and budget are the top issues in education, teachers and school leaders are eager to discover evidence-informed ideas that work in the classroom.

There are three things that teachers need to do well: mark work, plan lessons and teach students. The intention of *Mark. Plan. Teach.* is to encourage teachers to view their teaching process as a continuous cycle:

Each stage of the *Mark. Plan. Teach.* cycle informs the next; no stage exists in isolation. This book offers a range of strategies for each stage of the cycle, backed up by educational research and psychological perspectives, which will help shed light on why some strategies work better than others. The ideas will enable teachers to develop their classroom repertoire over a sustained period of time, reducing their workload and leaving them in no doubt that they are doing what is right for their students.

In *Mark. Plan. Teach.*, I promise to offer:

1. Tried-and-tested classroom ideas, supported with action research.

2. Teaching strategies based on cognitive processes, backed up by insights from leading psychologist, Dr Tim O'Brien.

3. Ideas that are accessible for every teacher, regardless of government fad or whim.

I pose questions that all teachers must ask of themselves to help them to manage their workload and begin to drive change within the education sector as a whole. Teachers need to take back control of their classroom domains and with *Mark. Plan. Teach.*, I want to offer a call to arms! Every teacher can learn to use classroom techniques that are steeped in evidence from research and psychology. By doing so, and adapting practice along the way, teachers can maximise students' potential, regardless of what league tables or 'expected progress' reports suggest. In this book, I will show you how to accomplish simple techniques in your classroom that you never thought were possible.

So, find yourself a quiet spot where you'll be uninterrupted, grab a cup of coffee and a pen, put your feet up and let me take you to a place where the complicated can be made simple and accessible for every teacher.

There is only one disclaimer; to use a phrase coined by educationalist Dylan Wiliam, 'everything works somewhere, and nothing works everywhere'. Context is king. I have used the ideas I present in this book throughout my career – in both stable and challenging institutions. However, the critical difference between how these ideas are applied is not just the school you are working in, but the teacher you are.

What makes a good teacher?

There are still many unanswered questions within the world of education. First and foremost, what makes a good teacher? How do we know if we're any good? Are we consistently the teacher we would want for ourselves? And how do these answers vary from school to school? A great teacher in a stable and affluent school is going to be working very differently to a great teacher working in a challenging school. And the rewards for the teacher and what a school can do to support them will also vary significantly.

The structure of a school building and all of its internal operations haven't changed very much over the past century. In secondary schools, the school bell generally still rings on the hour and every teacher and student must close their books and move on to another lesson or venue. Yet, how we learn as students – and as teachers – has shifted considerably over the past decade. We can now discover knowledge far beyond the walls of our own classroom, with information coming at teachers from every angle: the news, social media and from our colleagues at the chalkface. It is therefore critical that schools develop a common-sense approach to helping their teachers survive and thrive in the classroom.

Good teachers make a difference, but no one quite knows for sure what makes a good teacher. We only have our assumptions, and we should acknowledge that there is no single answer to being a great classroom practitioner. There are many roads to greatness in the classroom. Although we cannot ignore external agencies, we should acknowledge that whatever your teaching style, specialism or approach, if students enjoy your lessons, you get the results year-on-year and parents say they are 'delighted that you are teaching my child', then it works. So, keep doing what you are doing and have faith in your ability to change the lives of thousands of children.

However, in the teaching sector, a common trait we all share is the ability to reflect on our performance and to adapt our practice to the needs of our students. After all, there are many roads that lead to our school gates, with no route necessarily making you any better than the teacher next door to you.

There are many questions that I asked of myself in the nineties and still do, twenty years later. I know that every teacher at some point in their career wants to be better. Questioning your practice is essential if you are to build an awareness of where you are in your teaching now and which areas you need to develop further, so you can be the best teacher you can possibly be, no matter how experienced you are or what decade you find yourself teaching in.

Nevertheless, questioning your own practice is one thing, but having it questioned by others, particularly managers or third parties who have forgotten what it's like to teach a full day (or never knew in the first place), is quite another. Teachers in England, for example, have had to listen to countless politicians and experts advocate methods of teaching from overseas, comparing English, maths and science test scores from students in very different cultures and contexts, to then proclaim, 'this is what *our* teachers should be doing'. We find Shanghai Maths and direct instruction lessons being modelled by teachers from overseas in our own classrooms and professional development courses 'showcasing how we should all teach'.

Of course, there is nothing wrong with sharing best practice. In her book, *Cleverlands*, Lucy Crehan ends her epic journey of exploring the secrets of our education superpowers by arguing:

> 'To attribute these countries' enviable outcomes to culture and therefore dismiss their value as models would be a grave mistake. Culture can change. And it is schools and school systems that have the power to change it.' (Crehan, 2016)

However, it is my belief that we have the very best professionals in our classrooms already. Think about teachers working in challenging schools and very difficult circumstances, with judgements constantly being made about their schools and their backs against the wall; not everything they do is poor, nor should they believe that their work is not good enough.

We *need* teachers to work in challenging situations. We *need* to recognise that the work we do in all of our schools is already good, even if it could be better. What we really need to do to promote best practice is to provide sufficient time and funding to give our teachers the time to mark, plan and teach better and to reflect on their practice more regularly. Without that, our profession will always be on the back foot.

Mark. Plan. Teach. is especially dedicated to teachers working in challenging circumstances – those who have been forced to adopt gimmicks and fads for observers who are only fleetingly in their classroom. You know the ones – the managers who muster little respect, who spend less time in your classroom than it takes to write the lesson plan for that same blooming lesson! This book is for those teachers who wish to use evidence-based interventions that have the greatest impact on students, whilst avoiding government fads, and for those who only wish to focus on classroom strategies from the ground up. It is written and offered to you in the hope that it can help to inspire our next generation of classroom heroes.

We can be masters of our own destiny in whatever context and whatever country we are teaching. You reading this book can be the best teacher you can be, despite all the rhetoric, guff and external accountability. Our schools need you and more importantly, so do your students.

Educational research

There is no shortage of research being undertaken to help try to improve the quality of education provided in schools across the world. We now have Research Schools in England, defined as 'a network of schools who will support the use of evidence to improve teaching practice'. They are tasked with the mission to become a focal point for evidence-based practice in their region and to communicate, train, model and innovate methods for improvement (Education Endowment Foundation; EEF, 2017a).

You might think that after hundreds of years of teaching, we would have discovered rather more about the best ways for teachers to teach and students to learn, but somehow there appears to be more disagreement than agreement.

Reliability is extremely difficult to achieve in educational research. This is due to the very high numbers of variables involved and unavoidable levels of bias, in terms of the selection and the setup of experiments, the manipulation of subjective data and the communication of results, especially where an agency or think tank is keen to prove their hypothesis is correct.

While quantitative scientific research deals with data that is objective and reliably repeatable under identical conditions, qualitative educational research deals with subjective observations and opinions. However, to justify its conclusions, educational research often adopts techniques and methodologies that are based on sampling, surveys and scale-based ratings. These produce numerical data that can be subjected to statistical analysis, but this runs into the same problems of manipulation that we sometimes see in scientific research.

Some educational research involves the extended use of data-free case studies and ethnographic studies. While there is still potential for considerable bias in these, they can result in interesting, thought-provoking insights for further consideration. Meanwhile, a current controversial area of educational research is based in the area of neuroscience and cognitive psychology, which explores the biological process of learning. Unfortunately the 'scientific' data derived from such studies has sometimes been used to sell specific educational products into schools, while other findings have been misunderstood.

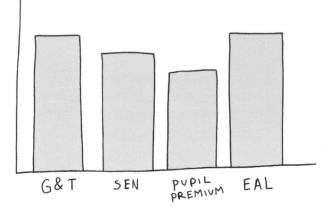

Yet despite all these pitfalls, reformers and governments impose policy based on data shared in research reports, which also feeds the media and fuels parental perceptions. It's very important to be aware of this at a time when the Department for Education (DfE) in England are busy reforming education based on research data that they have interpreted to suit their policies. Indeed, while in the past, policy arose out of the results of research, today it's often the other way around – research is undertaken to justify a particular policy.

As I write this introduction, the new Chartered College of Teaching in England aims to equip the profession with a teacher-led, evidence-based network for every teacher. You will know, as much as I and the people who are driving forward this new initiative, that there are no magic silver bullets in education that will instantly create better teachers and better students. However, we do need a teacher-led organisation within the sector that can at least point us in the right direction.

Perhaps all the problems inherent in conducting meaningful, reliable educational research explains why in hundreds of years of education provision, there is still little consensus as to what and how we should be teaching our students. While research in most other aspects of our lives has succeeded in producing a sense of progress, the current political policy in England is that we need to go back to traditional approaches to education that have little to do with the future learning needs of our children.

Why has the educational research that has been undertaken failed to provide us with any widely accepted sense that we have discovered new and improved ways of educating our students? Is there anything to suggest that future research will do any better? In his book *Open: How We'll Work, Live and Learn in the Future*, David Price says that 'formal education has adopted an "inside-out" mindset – schools and colleges have usually been organised around the needs of educators, not the learners' (Price, 2013).

If all this makes us question educational research, then what it has achieved is to encourage us to examine and discuss existing practice, raise questions and search for possible answers. The evidence it produces points the way to new or emerging practices and methodologies that might, in certain situations, prove to be worthwhile for certain groups of the student population.

Often, those who benefit most from research are the individuals who have actually been involved in collecting and analysing the data – indeed it's probably the best form of CPD there is. This is a positive thing, just as long as it's understood that it isn't necessarily going to provide any guarantee or certainty of improvement for everyone.

The future of government lies in being transparent, but with that transparency comes accountability. Teachers yearn for a culture of classroom practice where they are free to share and be trusted. They want a profession where they are also participating with passion and purpose to enable deep and powerful learning to happen.

In today's culture, it takes a brave school leader to protect their staff from external pressures, to reduce workload and to ignore various policies, in a climate of high accountability, which (supposedly) guarantees better student outcomes. If we are to do things that really work in schools, then we need to start using one another's experiences in the classroom as evidence in itself. If we want to do great work, we need to enable teachers to meet more regularly to share ideas about what is working with their students. As Price says:

> 'Allowing everyone the freedom to follow their interests sends an important message: that good ideas can be found anywhere, by anyone.' (Price, 2013)

As a deputy headteacher, I started to conduct my own research into a coaching methodology and dialogue to replace formal lesson observations in my school. This soon developed into wider research looking at what common traits can be found in effective teachers and what evidence-based strategies they use. The outcome was a short policy designed to build consistency across the school and this was the beginning of the *Mark. Plan. Teach.* framework. Our school leadership team had weekly conversations about this framework, tinkering with it and debating ideas with all staff every month before it finally became a one page summary document that communicated expectations to all teachers and aimed to ensure consistency in all classrooms.

Each and every section of this book, therefore, builds upon every single conversation I've had in my school over the past three years. Of course, the *Mark. Plan. Teach.* methodology also contains my experience of over 20,000 lessons taught, lessons I have observed from over 1,000 teachers in London, as well as the authors I reference throughout this book and list in the bibliography on p. 176. This book is my 'action research'. It shares my experiences of the classroom and is written to provoke, challenge and inspire every teacher.

Mark. Plan. Teach. offers my field notes to the rest of the profession.

How to use this book

I have written **Mark. Plan. Teach.** in such a way that it can be read from start to finish to mirror the teaching process. The three sections each present ideas relating to one aspect of this process, all the while acknowledging how each stage of the cycle informs the next and cannot exist in isolation. Remember:

Of course, each section can also be read and put into practice independently, as can each individual idea. Equally, each section and each idea can be redesigned into a professional development session to train staff.

What will I find in each section?

Each section is divided into **ten** tried-and-tested ideas that can be implemented in the classroom. The ideas all begin with an 'idea snapshot', which provides an overview of the concept. Use these snapshots to dip in and out of the book and find the ideas and strategies you are looking for. You can easily pick out these snapshots by keeping an eye out for the camera icon as you flick through the book. Each section of the book ends with a short summary that provides a neat recap of all the ideas. Consider these summaries as essential synopses of the strategies in each section.

Each idea I present is supported by educational research or a psychological perspective, which helps to explain **how** and **why** the idea works. Look out for the following at the end of each idea:

Evidence

These sections draw upon a wide range of educational research relating to the ideas and how and why they work. However, regardless of this evidence, remember that context is everything and I am not suggesting that any of these ideas will work perfectly in *all* school settings and circumstances.

Psychology

In these sections, Dr Tim O'Brien, Visiting Fellow in Psychology and Human Development at UCL Institute of Education, focuses on particular aspects of my ideas and offers perspectives that consider the psychological processes behind the ideas. If you wish to reference anything from these sections in your own writing, please reference the section like this: (for example) O'Brien, T. (2017), 'Psychology and reflection', in R. M. McGill, *Mark. Plan. Teach.*, London: Bloomsbury.

Who is this book for?

Throughout the three decades that I've been working in schools – yes, I did start teaching in the 1990s when banda machines were the talk of the staffroom – I have been asked to implement countless strategies in my classroom, some of which haven't stood the test of time. Some training sessions have advocated providing trails of evidence for watchdogs, such as verbal feedback stamps, as well as 'research-informed' strategies that have later turned out to lack rigour and evidence. Today, we'd call this 'fake news'.

This book is for every teacher. I hope that by sharing some of my tried-and-tested strategies and supporting these with evidence and psychological perspectives, you will be tempted to apply some of them in your own classroom. This book is also for every leader of teaching and learning, who shares ideas with larger groups of teachers. It can be used as a training manual in professional development sessions to equip every teacher with classroom strategies for the very next day. For the past ten years, I have been working in very challenging school settings, where classroom ideas are difficult to implement across an entire school. We know that 'collective teacher efficacy' (see Section 3, Idea 3, p. 128) has a huge impact on student outcomes, but any idea – including those shared in *Mark. Plan. Teach.* – will only be as effective as the teacher who delivers them. Gone are the days of monotony and one size fits all. Teachers and schools need to be able to cherry pick strategies that work for them and their students, so use these ideas as a platform for inspiration, discussion and provocation with your colleagues.

Whoever you are, all I ask is for you to remember that context is king with everything you read in this book. I offer ideas that can stand the test of time, regardless of subject or setting. It is my intention to share every ounce of knowledge I have with you. I hope you enjoy the read and that this becomes a well-thumbed book on your desk.

No matter how hard you look...

...you will NOT find the word 'Ofsted' in this book, other than in this sentence*. As in most of my writing, I will refer to this watchdog by my preferred nickname: the 'Grim Reaper'!

*and for accurate referencing.

Section 1:
MARK.

A long time ago, in a school far away (when I was less experienced)... I found marking to be a real burden. I never understood the value of assessment, and verbal and written feedback was something I just did. Over the last decade, research and the growth of social media for teachers' professional development have exposed misguided practice and allowed teachers and schools to work collaboratively outside of their silos. In this new epoch, I have academic research and evidence in the palm of my hand to help better understand how assessment and feedback can make the greatest difference to a student's progress.

Assessment, feedback and marking form a crucial part of every teacher's daily routine, regardless of their experience, the subject they teach, or the ability and age range of their students. The importance of high-quality feedback has been evidenced by many academic studies and is notably outlined by Professor John Hattie in his book *Visible Learning for Teachers*. Hattie shares the benefits of a rigorous approach to marking and feedback, including the fact that assessing students helps teachers to learn about their own impact. This can be seen in everyday classrooms where students are thriving and progress is on an upward trajectory as a result of the quality of what teachers do on a daily basis.

'As a professional, it is critical to know thy impact. It may seem ironic, but the more teachers seek feedback about their own impact, the more benefits accrue to their students.' (Hattie, 2012)

Nevertheless, every teacher has struggled with their marking load at some point in their career; it's an occupational hazard. We know there is a need for greater research in this area to help alleviate the burden on teachers. So, why do we need to mark students' work? And what is the best way to go about it?

I write this section of **Mark. Plan. Teach.** with the important yet challenging nature of assessment, feedback and marking in mind. I distil tried-and-tested gems and expose several gimmicks that I believe you can dispense with to equip you with strategies for marking that will reduce workload and increase classroom impact.

What is the purpose of assessment, feedback and marking?

Assessment, feedback and marking have three purposes:

1. Students act on feedback to make progress over time.

2. They inform future planning and teaching.

3. Students learn to value hard work and the quality of the work they produce.

Of course, we will come across more purposes in this section of the book, but for this introduction, let's just consider the above.

Making progress

Marking is a continuum between teacher and student, and student and teacher. It should be a dialogue, written or spoken, and something that students use to understand better and try to improve. The aim of assessing work effectively is to get students to engage with the feedback in whatever form it is presented, and then take action in order to improve their learning. Ultimately, assessment and marking should enable students to act on feedback received. We can therefore accept that a feedback-loop, which helps the student to improve each time, is critical to a student's success.

Assessment and feedback seek to highlight those elements of marking that have the greatest impact on learning, namely:

*   Sharing the key marking points (the success criteria). A student is much more likely to be successful if they know where they are going and how to get there. This is what John Hattie labels as 'teacher clarity' in his study of over 800 meta-analyses relating to achievement (Hattie, 2009). I call 'teacher clarity' 'stickability', or what knowledge, skills and understanding students must leave the classroom with and bring back to the next lesson (see Section 2, Idea 4, p. 78).

*   Giving clear feedback to students about their work, for example comments-only marking or even just verbal feedback, but crucially making sure they *respond* to your marking by correcting their work or re-doing it using your comments to guide them

to a higher standard. A simple way to achieve this is by using an excellent strategy to reduce workload and increase impact: the yellow box (see Section 1, Idea 3, p. 17).

If we can keep these elements at the forefront of our minds, our marking will be more focused and efficient and will help our students to progress.

Informing teaching

Consider marking from the basis of informing the teacher to be even better than before, not just the students. Research does say that the *quality* of the teacher makes the greatest difference to a child. It says nothing about how much or how little marking we should do and how hard we should work at it.

Report after report and survey after survey show that teachers are working in excess of 50 hours every week to keep on top of their workload. The workforce experiences common mental health conditions: according to a survey in 2014 by the Education Support Partnership (previously the Teacher Support Network Group), '88% [of teachers polled] said they suffered from stress, 72% anxiety and 45% had depression' and '13% quit their job' as a result (Education Support Partnership, 2014).

So why have we created an unmanageable beast that is driving teachers to leave the profession or, worse, to depression, particularly when research suggests our focus should be on quality of teaching, not quantity of marking?

Marking will tell you how effective your teaching has been and whether your students have grasped the concepts and developed the skills required by your assessment framework. It will also show you the progress your students have made over time. This will then inform whether you need to go back and re-teach any aspects of the curriculum (see Section 1, Idea 6, p. 34), whether you need to change how you are teaching them and what you could teach your students next. Marking will help you understand the what, how and why of teaching (see Section 1, Idea 2, p. 13) and lead to a quality first teaching approach, which will ensure you are teaching your students in the best way possible.

The value of hard work

In schools where teachers are contracted to teach for 90% of their time, or in difficult schools where behaviour is challenging, finding any free time to mark outside of the classroom is a poisoned chalice. I personally believe that the hard work should be in the classroom, not away from it. Live-marking offers a solution (see Section 1, Idea 3, p. 17), but we should also remember that, when it comes to marking, the hard work should be for the person receiving the feedback and not for the person providing the assessment.

Not only should your students engage with and respond to your feedback, but the onus should be on them to reflect on their own work, be able to recognise its flaws and fix them before you've even seen it! (See Section 1, Idea 7, p. 38.) Encourage a culture of self- and peer-assessment in your classroom (see Section 1, Idea 9, p. 45) and refuse to mark anything that isn't up to standard! (See Section 1, Idea 10, p. 50.) This will save you time and help your students take control of their own learning and progress.

Verbal feedback

In a blog post, Roy Blatchford, Founding Director of the National Education Trust, likens observing teachers making mistakes in the classroom to the surgeons who once removed a benign melanoma from his wrist:

> 'The lead surgeon began cutting precisely then passed over the scalpel to one of his juniors. Within thirty seconds he seized it back, clearly not content with the direction of the incision [...] Ever since that moment [...] I have rarely observed a lesson without interacting in some way.' (Blatchford, 2015)

Could the same be said for assessment? If we see a student going off on the wrong track, should we intervene? I would like to suggest that we should. I believe that there is a greater need for verbal feedback as the default mechanism for marking so we can give immediate feedback that will aid students in the lesson, rather than weeks later when a teacher has finally found time to provide written feedback.

Verbal feedback would also help combat workload, teacher-health issues and ensure feedback is incisive, as well as 'meaningful', 'manageable' and 'motivating', as research published by the DfE suggests it should be (DfE, 2016; see Section 1, Idea 4, Evidence, p. 26). It would reduce the burden of marking in exchange for sharing initial feedback, mark schemes and common errors, and even help a teacher become better at what they are teaching.

Issues at whole-school level

However, there are two problems that our schools and school leaders face when trying to improve assessment, feedback and marking. Examination boards and school inspections both impact on even the smartest teaching and learning policies designed to eradicate the marking burden.

Firstly, no matter how hard schools try to design a simple marking policy, there will be some teachers – particularly those teaching examination classes in Years 6 and 11 – who, in spite of their best efforts to follow school policy, will be trumped by external examination requirements asking teachers to mark drafts, redrafts and provide endless commentary.

The second issue is more serious for schools. At the time of writing, teaching and learning policies – or more specifically, marking policies – are not statutory law (DfE, 2014a). Schools are not required to have one or publish one for parents. Obviously every school hopes to communicate how students' work will be marked and how often, and no school would want to alienate their students and parents by keeping assessment a secret – this would be the polar opposite of 'teacher clarity'. However, schools are setting themselves up to fail – and don't even know it – if external partners who quality assure teaching and learning test what non-statutory policies say versus what is happening and then hold schools to account for it!

Here's how it happens:

1. The school creates, consults and publishes a teaching and learning policy for staff, students and parents.

2. Teachers are trained – and then expected to mark – according to a set frequency or framework.

3. School leaders monitor who is following the system well and who is not, then tweak it and repeat.

4. Parents complain that a policy is not being followed.

5. Students remain complacent regardless.

6. The most able students make progress and the most disadvantaged children actually need more than a marking policy to help them understand why schooling is important to their future outcomes.

7. Over time, impending school inspections raise anxiety and school leaders start to beat teachers over the head with a stick.

8. Teachers get stressed. They either pull their socks up and sustain a heavy workload for a period of time or buckle under the strain.

9. Capability ensues as school leaders expect to be measured according to external partner methodologies and binary measures.

10. The result? Stressed-out teachers, headless school leaders and school inspectors judging how well schools can implement non-statutory policy.

It's a mindless cycle that leads to more cynicism and confusion.

So what's the solution?

Schools should create a simple marking policy if they have to. My suggestions are:

- Teachers must have a secure overview of the starting points of their students and their pathways (see Section 1, Idea 1, p. 6).

- Assessment must use diagnostic feedback as a default process for improvement (see Section 1, Idea 2, p. 13).

- Marking must be regular and proportionate to curriculum time (see Section 1, Idea 4, p. 23).

We should also remember that the value of organisations, school leaders and teachers assessing the quality of marking from books alone is limited. It is only one way to gauge student progress and is susceptible to interpretation and serious weaknesses if not conducted reliably (see Section 1, Idea 8, p. 41).

Instead, we could raise the profile of verbal feedback, for example, and trust that if a student can demonstrate specific knowledge or skills by the end of a scheme of work, feedback has taken place, a student has acted upon it and progress has been made.

That is a school I'd like to work in.

A secure overview

IDEA 1

IDEA SNAPSHOT

Before you set an assessment and then sit down to mark it, you should first consider where you are in the curriculum and the purpose of setting and marking this specific piece of work. Think about the starting point, progress and context of each student. This 'secure overview' will inform how you spend time marking to improve teaching, learning and assessment.

John Hattie's research suggests that 'goal setting' has a significant impact (d=0.60) on student outcomes because it helps students see the 'bigger picture' in their learning (Hattie, 2009). Imagine a map that is directing you where to go, with countless options ahead of you informing how you might get there. It is vital to have this 'bigger picture' in place as part of curriculum planning and assessment, not only so that students understand where they are going, but so teachers have a secure grasp of what needs to be taught and assessed.

In his book *The Slightly Awesome Teacher*, Dominic Salles suggests that setting goals is 'largely about workload and time management – getting through the curriculum' (Salles, 2016). As much as it saddens me to write it here in black and white, I agree.

Teachers are time poor and in constant conflict between:

- what they would like to teach
- what they have to teach
- what they have to evidence for external stakeholders.

Nevertheless, if we start everything we do with the end outcome in mind, surely we are at least in a stronger position as teachers? This will lead to smarter assessment, reduced workload and better outcomes for the students.

The difficulty for a school, and any individual teacher, is not knowing whether your colleague is doing exactly the same as you with the same students in the classroom next door. If 'Mr Can't Be Bothered' doesn't share lesson objectives and goals, or if 'Mrs Conscientious' insists that every student writes lesson objectives from the board into their exercise books, then you will have a problem too.

Teacher expectations and routines vary and there is scope for students to become confused between one teacher's expectations and another's. In any school, students will find the gaps – opportunities to misbehave or escape work – and many readers will nod their heads in agreement when I say how many times my colleagues have had students complain, 'But Miss, Mr McGill doesn't ask us to write down lesson objectives. Why do we have to copy them down in your lessons?'.

So how does any school address this if they want their teachers to be autonomous, yet consistent across the school? Well, it's a difficult question to answer and the context of the individual school will apply.

The solution? Teach in a way that works for you and your students. If it works in the grand scheme of things, should we really worry about whether students are writing, speaking, reading or listening to the learning objectives?

Share the objectives with students and make sure they understand them in the context of 'the bigger picture' of their learning, but do not allow yourself to become bogged down in the details of 'how you communicate' them to students and 'how students should demonstrate' that they know what they are supposed to be learning. Let's just get them learning!

Marking and feedback

So once we have a secure overview of the curriculum plan, what can school leaders and, more importantly, school teachers do with it in terms of marking and feedback?

Both the individual teacher's and whole school's approach to marking and feedback need to be well thought out, of high quality and appropriate for the individual school and setting. When marking and feedback is a regular routine in the classroom, it is always apparent: work is of a higher quality; students take more time over their work; work is better organised; students are able to talk about their learning and they have more opportunities to progress.

In my current place of work at the time of writing, the teachers developed a teaching and learning policy over a sustained period of 18 months. The policy – which was no flash in the pan – was consulted on at all levels and became a training manual with the section on marking feeding into CPD sessions and department meetings to help teachers assess accurately and coherently.

But when the Grim Reaper arrived, they ignored it! All they cared about was consistency and impact across the school. 18 months of staff training, consultation and staff development – evidence, in my opinion – was not used as evidence in a school inspection. Ironic, I know!

The crux of the matter is that once you have a secure overview of the curriculum plan, you can mark all work with this in mind in order to inform whether your students have learnt what they have been taught and if not, what they need to do to get there. This means that ALL your marking will have an impact on student outcomes and will eliminate any needless work on your part, reducing your workload and maximising your impact as a teacher!

Why not try my **5 Minute Marking Plan** to help you do this? The Plan seeks to highlight those elements of marking that have the greatest impact on learning, including sharing the key marking points, because a student is much more likely to be successful if they know where they are going. The Plan also underlines the importance of ensuring that students respond to your marking by correcting their work or re-doing it in order to guide them to a higher standard.

Find my 5 Minute Marking Plan here:

www.teachertoolkit.co.uk/2013/07/01/5-minute-marking-plan-2

Knowing your students

How well do teachers know their students? This is a standout feature of teachers who have great relationships and also know their students' data, including their prior starting points and current pathways. However, this is incredibly difficult to achieve, particularly for secondary teachers who may teach in excess of 450 students per week!

So how can you know your students personally, as well as their performance? Firstly, I am a traditional teacher from the old school of thought, where relationships between teacher and student trump any school policy, behaviour strategy or anything else we do in schools. However, over the past decade, schools and the way we teach have become more and more sophisticated, with data increasingly prominent in our conversations with young people. As a result, everything I do as a teacher is richer, more efficient and more effective because I am better informed regarding how students are performing. This means the relationships I have with my students are more powerful and meaningful when a) a good relationship with them is in place and b) I can present useful data to my students to help them progress, which also enables me to understand their progress better, when, for example, live-marking (see Section 1, Idea 3, p. 17).

It is this data that will allow teachers to build a secure overview of the starting points, progress and context of all students in the classroom, which is a huge help when marking.

This data may involve the following:

1. Information provided from previous schools or classes should be fully understood and used for planning. This includes:

    a. prior attainment data from primary school

    b. reading age

    c. how the student is doing in your subject compared to others

    d. how the student has done in the subject prior to you teaching them

    e. other vital information such as whether the student has English as an additional language (EAL), special educational needs and disabilities (SEND) or is gifted and talented (G&T).

2. Teachers should understand the student's overall strengths and weaknesses. In examination courses, a personalised learning checklist can often provide students with an overview of the course content and areas for assessment. This is an excellent signal that a teacher has planned well and intends on having a secure overview of every student in front of them.

3. Teachers should also be aware of the context of each class from:

   a. the relationships teachers form with students, in line with behaviour or learning policy

   b. making at least a mental note of announcements about student welfare

   c. liaising with relevant pastoral teams and agencies where necessary to muster a deeper overview of the student; this is vital when working with disadvantaged or vulnerable students.

If we use the following simple step-by-step chart, we can build a secure overview of every student in our classrooms:

Step 1	Step 2	Step 3
Prior attainment and results	**Students' place in your course**	**Knowing your classes and kids**
What is it? • Results • Literacy • SEND/EAL • G&T	**What is it?** • Student strengths and weaknesses • Personalised learning checklists • Class tracking • Target groups	**What is it?** • Behaviour • Attendance • Pastoral issues • Likes and interests
Examples of where we can find this information: • Whole-school datasets • Attainment data from feeder early years or primary settings • Attainment data from colleagues	**Examples of where we can find this information:** • Your marking and feedback • Your class datasets • Your observations in class	**Examples of where we can find this information:** • Your relationships with students and parents • School briefings, bulletins and end-of-day reports • Colleagues, pastoral teams and agencies

Remember: a student's context rarely means you should adjust your aspirations of what they can achieve. High expectations are critical in the classroom, yet sometimes there are events in a student's life that make it very hard for them to learn. These students are the exception, not the rule, but we should never give up on them. I would rarely adjust my expectations for any child unless there were exceptional circumstances, for example a safeguarding issue is known and having the child in school is more important than asking them to complete a task.

Now you have a secure overview of every student in your class, make sure you keep this in mind when you are marking their work. This will help you to focus on the key marking points that will really make a difference to the learning of the individual student and guide them personally to a higher standard of learning. Again, this will not only reduce any unnecessary work on your part but also help to ensure that every single piece of marking you do has a direct impact on your students' learning!

Reflecting on your marking and feedback

Reflecting upon the value of marking and feedback to improve your own teaching is not a cardinal sin. Developing your understanding of the purpose of high-quality, focused marking and feedback and the way you incorporate this into your daily practice is an essential part of being a teacher. It will not disappear. Teachers will always need to mark students' work and it will be the bane of anyone's career if not done with aplomb.

Whether you are a class teacher looking to develop your practice or you are a school leader responsible for delivering CPD training for marking and feedback, *Bloomsbury CPD Library: Marking and Feedback* by Sarah Findlater provides an excellent methodology for assessment (Findlater, 2016):

Stage 1 Assess

Take the self-assessment questionnaire provided in Findlater's book to help reflect on what you already know and identify areas for improvement.

Stage 2 Improve

Consider what key theorists are saying about the different types of marking and feedback and how to put them into practice in the classroom.

NOTE: There are several key influencers and assessment theorists in education who are shaping the assessment dialogue. For example, assessing without levels advocate, Daisy Christodoulou, writes in an essay for think tank Policy Exchange:

'... multiple-choice questions can be very powerful when used for classroom formative assessment, because the existence of several wrong options allows the teacher to identify who has grasped a new concept, and who is still labouring under a common misconception.' (Christodoulou, 2015)

But how many of these influencers and theorists have recently marked a full class-set of books? I know this is a weak argument but I am not throwing my toys out of the pram here and in fact, I am not even arguing. Academic research is essential, yet teachers know better than anyone else about what works in the classroom; we just do not necessarily have the time to engage with research or the privilege to access it. It is vital that teachers are 'research rich' or at least informed, so we need to have experts – outside of the classroom – who can work on academic studies and research for the greater good. However, we must all remember that context is king.

Stage 3 Evaluate

Think about how you have improved your marking so far. When did you last look at another teacher's set of books or the book of a student you teach to understand what deal they are getting elsewhere? This is a really powerful CPD exercise for any teacher. Not all teachers will become 'teacher-researchers' but every teacher can still become research rich if we facilitate opportunities within our own schools for teachers to learn from one another. Appointed 'research leads' could promote 'what works' and dispel myths (if given time and resources as part of their working responsibility). Only this can see us all improve the marking frenzy.

Stage 4 Excel

Continue to improve and embed good practice in the classroom and the rest of the school. Once we curate opportunities for teachers to mark during the day – by reducing the need for written feedback and replacing this with verbal feedback – as well as for teachers to come together to discuss assessment, marking and feedback, only then can we continue to improve and embed good practice in the classroom as well as in the rest of the school.

Stage 5 Developing others

Begin training others in school. No one can really master the art of marking, but your awareness of assessment strategies and techniques to help reduce workload and improve impact must be considered. External training can be expensive and may not deliver the outcomes you are hoping for, so it is vital that in-house expertise is cultivated.

Who better to lead staff training than you? Whether it is one training session or a term's worth of training sessions, the advice in Findlater's book should help you to get started with planning and implementing your own CPD in your school.

Psychology and...
a secure overview

In these Psychology sections, Dr Tim O'Brien, Visiting Fellow in Psychology and Human Development at UCL Institute of Education, will focus on a particular aspect in each of Ross' ideas and offer a psychological perspective.

Ross proposes that a secure overview allows a teacher to develop a secure base for teaching. They know where the students are in terms of their learning and where they are heading. This is vital. One critique of the current educational climate is that it has become obsessed with data. There is value in gathering data for a purpose but children and young people are not data – they are humans with vulnerabilities and needs. The needs of some students are evident to a teacher whilst other students develop strategies to camouflage certain needs. I propose that a secure overview should also include an awareness of psychological needs. When a teacher is aware of psychological needs, it enables students to develop a more secure base for learning.

One psychological need I shall consider here, varying in nature from individual to individual, is the need to feel a sense of belonging. Feeling that you belong creates a sense of emotional security and self-validity. So, how can you help a student feel or know that they belong in your classroom? At the risk of stating the obvious, it is a classroom and therefore access to learning is critical. Consider how you can adapt what you think, feel and do to increase the possibilities of removing barriers to learning – and not only for those students identified as experiencing SEND. If a student believes they can learn in your classroom, and knows that their learning will be acknowledged, they are more likely to feel that they belong there. Learning is an emotional as well as a cognitive activity, and recognition of the emotional aspects of learning, such as persistence and curiosity, can also create a sense of belonging. There are also strategies that can enhance an individual's sense of belonging when they are in a group. For example, when talking to the whole class, a teacher can openly communicate that they have high expectations for all students. Creating a sense of belonging is a psychological enabler for learning.

A student's sense of belonging can be nurtured, reinforced or amplified when they have a positive relationship with their teacher. Relationships are the heartbeats of pedagogy. Relationships matter – especially as research highlights that teachers will be involved in over one thousand interpersonal contacts every single day (Holmes, 2005). Realistically, for a teacher, it may be easier to develop positive relationships with some students more than others. So, make a conscious effort to notice the nature and quality of your interactions with all students. It is also worth being aware that research indicates that when teachers develop positive relationships with students, it is not only beneficial to the students – it also has an unambiguously positive impact on teacher wellbeing.

Not yet...

IDEA SNAPSHOT

Use the powerful words 'not yet' in your marking to cut through complex grading systems and form a simple assessment framework that will motivate students to improve their learning and develop a growth mindset.

Summative marking means evaluating a piece of work according to a success criteria and giving it a grade. **Formative marking**, on the other hand, is not about giving a grade, but rather providing commentary on the level the student is working at in order to improve learning. Despite this distinction, formative and summative marking are things that every teacher must do, and both often require the use of multiple assessment frameworks. Understanding multiple assessment frameworks is therefore critical, and communicating a grading system to students to help them understand the work they are doing, and more importantly, why they are doing it, is fundamental practice in the classroom.

When assessing students' work either summatively or formatively, you must think about how you are going to feed back. What grading criteria will you share? There are countless grading systems across the world and multiple frameworks in the UK alone. At Key Stage 3 in England, for example, at the time of writing, the range of assessment is more disjointed than it ever has been. So stage, age, subject and country aside, how should we as teachers create a system where we can be masters of the classroom for the benefit of our students?

Obviously your school, department or subject will have an agreed system for teachers to use. I sincerely hope they do anyway. But you must also consider how well your students understand it. After all, they are the ones that need to know what it all means and how to improve, right?

So let's think about it this way: if you created a new project and scheme of learning from the outset that had no assessment framework to start with, what would you do and where would you go? Hopefully you will agree that the design of the curriculum comes first, but without an assessment framework, it is difficult for the teacher, never mind the students, to gauge performance and progress.

I propose that, as a starting point, both summative and formative marking should be **diagnostic**, namely we should make it clear to the student how to improve the piece of work and overall learning, rather than simply giving them a grade. This will help to remove the culture where thousands of students are transfixed on their grade and not on what they need to do to improve. If we can shift this approach, we can also improve teachers' workload.

Using the words 'not yet'

One great strategy for diagnostic marking is using the two words 'not yet'. This is a fabulous method promoted by Professor Carol Dweck, who advocates the use of a 'Not Yet' grade. For Dweck, a fail grade tells a student, 'I'm nothing; I'm nowhere', but if they receive the grade 'Not Yet', they will understand that they are on a learning curve that gives a path into the future. Dweck asks, 'How are we raising our children? Are we raising them for *now* instead of *yet*? Are we raising kids who are obsessed with getting As?'

According to Dweck, if we feed back wisely, praising students because of their efforts rather than their outcomes, we can develop a growth mindset culture in our students. Young people who engage show 'their effort, their strategies, their focus, their perseverance, their improvement […] Just the words "yet" or "not yet" […] give kids greater confidence [and] create persistence.' (Dweck, 2014)

The 'not yet' approach can be used in written feedback, but it is just as effective in verbal feedback. Try marking the first piece of work students produce in the morning with a simple 'not yet because…' and see the immediate effect. You can't use this technique in your back garden on a sunny day, so why not leave your books at school and provide immediate, meaningful and motivating feedback based on Dweck's research? It's only your senior leadership team and the 'observer police' who want to see reams and reams of written feedback. It shows you are working hard. But if it's not required, then why waste the time? Give students the feedback they deserve, today.

Where is the best place for me to mark?

Being a reflective practitioner will help you answer this one. You might want to get all your marking done in school, either in your classroom, the staffroom or an empty office, so you don't have to take your work home with you. Or you might find it easier to mark at home in a quiet space that allows you to focus without the distractions you may get at school. We all have our own preferred space and time to work. *You* must choose the environment, the time and the space where *you* can get marking done.

Using 'not yet' to evaluate and improve your teaching

In my teaching career, I have found that marking for a new term – whether this is before or immediately after a holiday period – is a great way to use the 'not yet' method of diagnostic marking. I look back at my students' targets from the previous term and try to specify whether they have achieved targets set or whether they are 'not yet' there. This signposts students' progress and can be a keystone for planning the term ahead. For the first lesson back after a period apart, consider what students have forgotten and what path you need to take them on next.

When evaluating the quality of teaching, learning and assessment, the following three things should be taken into consideration:

1. The **what** of teaching, namely what is being taught and when. This is determined by the curriculum and the curriculum should of course trump everything else.

2. The **how** of learning, namely the delivery that makes learning possible. How do we translate the curriculum into the classroom?

3. The **why** of teaching, namely why we are teaching the content and why we are teaching it in this way.

The **why** of teaching is the cognition process of lesson planning but it is often the last aspect on the minds of busy, time-poor teachers and is left behind in many of our day-to-day decisions in the classroom. 'I have lots of time to think about assessment and planning,' said no teacher, ever.

But it shouldn't be like this! If we can all consider the **why** of teaching, we may be able to equip ourselves, as well as our students, to acquire mastery in the classroom. Using the 'not yet' marking approach can be the perfect place to start. Once you know whether your students have achieved their targets, or whether they are 'not yet' there, you can plan which content to teach next term, how you are going to teach it and understand and explain to students the reasons why. See Section 2, Idea 2, p. 66 for more on lesson planning based on the **why** of teaching.

EVIDENCE

In her research paper, 'Even Geniuses Work Hard', Professor Carol Dweck argues that meaningful feedback on difficult classwork can motivate 'students to love challenges, to enjoy effort, to be resilient, and to value their own improvement'. This can all be achieved with the simple word 'yet'. Dweck states that 'yet' 'should be used frequently in every classroom. Whenever students say they can't do something or are not good at something, the teacher should add "yet"' (Dweck, 2010).

In terms of motivation levels, we want students to develop their own habits of self-regulation, and there is compelling evidence that people can learn, and therefore be taught, how to improve their levels of self-control.

Tougher Minds – a programme for learning and study to help anybody enhance their personal performance – has been proven to dramatically improve all aspects of school work, including learning, homework, concentration, behaviour, exam performance and extra curricular sport; all useful habits students should develop.

In a research project conducted by Tougher Minds in a school in which I have worked, the Tougher Minds performance psychology programme was piloted. It was designed to increase knowledge and understanding of self-control among participating students and help them to develop better habits of self-control. The aim was to develop young people who were empowered to take more control over their behaviour and learning at school, and in their broader lives.

The methodology used a randomly assigned Year 7 tutor group engaged in a seven-week intervention. A comparison Year 7 group was also selected. This group did not receive the intervention, but data was collected about their behaviour, before and after the intervention, concurrently with the students who did receive the intervention. The findings showed that the students who participated in the Tougher Minds programme developed a better understanding of self-control and were better able to deploy sophisticated self-control strategies than those who did not participate in the programme.

This evidence shows that it is possible to teach students how to improve their self-control and therefore to regulate their own motivation levels. So, start by using the simple word 'yet' and see where it takes you and your students in developing a growth mindset and improving learning.

Live-marking

IDEA SNAPSHOT

Over the years, I've used 'live-marking' – marking in lesson time with the student by my side – to embed formative assessment in my classroom and reduce the workload burden. Why not try it to see if it works for you too?

 llow me to explain how live-marking can be managed and what impact it can have. Teachers are bombarded with marking because it is central to their role, and some teachers and schools yearn to mark every piece of work and record written feedback for the 'marking police'. These folk come disguised as fleeting observers who seek no context about the teacher or student and who flit in and out of classrooms in the blink of an eye and the flick through a book. Parents also expect to see reams of written feedback on their children's work.

It is therefore more necessary than ever that schools have a clear feedback policy that is communicated to students, parents and colleagues so that marking is manageable and adds value. We know that feedback is one of the most effective ways to improve learning, but we should stipulate that not everything can be – or should be (see Section 1, Idea 10, p. 50) – marked.

I've been live-marking in all my lessons. It is a technique that is hard taught and hard earned but it does have many advantages. It does not always have to be written and can be verbal, and there is the benefit of it being there and then in the classroom, rather than two or three weeks later or, worse, when it is too late to adjust decision making during the learning process.

A research paper was published in April 2016 by the University of Oxford and the EEF, based on survey results from 1,382 practising teachers in 1,012 schools in the maintained sector in England (Elliott et al., 2016). The report found that evidence focused on written marking is of poor quality and that teachers and school leaders should create a marking policy that is effective, sustainable and time efficient. The report looked at seven different aspects of marking and considered the evidence and research currently available in the UK and internationally in relation to each.

The seven aspects were:

1. 'Grading'
2. 'Corrections'
3. 'Thoroughness'
4. 'Pupil responses'
5. 'Creating a dialogue'
6. 'Targets'
7. 'Frequency and speed'.

I will elaborate on three of these seven aspects – 'corrections', 'creating a dialogue' and 'frequency and speed' – in terms of live-marking and how they relate to giving feedback to students in the classroom.

'Corrections'

The EEF report says, 'when marking a piece of work, it may feel logical and efficient to provide students with the right answer'. The report then looks at the evidence that discusses how valuable this really is and considers other methods of pointing out and correcting errors when marking student work.

Live-marking can help discourage teachers from providing students with the answers or correcting every single error in a piece of work. Colleagues in my current school at the time of writing use the yellow box methodology when live-marking to support this. The yellow box is a more targeted approach to marking that ensures teachers and students focus on a specific area of the work (rather than the entire piece), that encourages teachers' feedback to be diagnostic and support improvement (rather than help students create a final product in every activity), and that reduces teachers' workload. See the box on the opposite page for an explanation of how this technique works.

'Creating a dialogue'

The EEF report discusses 'triple impact marking' (the teacher gives written feedback on a piece of work, the student responds to this feedback and the teacher then responds to this in turn) and 'dialogic marking' (where a written conversation develops between teachers and students). I do not expect any teacher to mark redrafted work. Does your school? If so, why should we insist that teachers mark the same work twice if we assume the average secondary school teacher has 300-500 students per week? It is an impossible ask and we must be realistic about workload and the level of impact that can be made from re-marking students' work.

Although the EEF report concludes that there is 'some promise underpinning the idea of creating a dialogue' and that more research is required to test this, I have been using live-marking to put a greater emphasis on verbal dialogue that is scripted and targeted to help students improve their work. This means that students can instantly act upon the feedback, all the while significantly reducing written marking for the

The yellow box

Choose one area of a student's work to mark – just one section – and draw a yellow box around it. Mark it well and in detail, offering feedback (verbally or in writing) that is sophisticated and, above all, specific and diagnostic (see Section 1, Idea 2, p. 13). Avoid assessing the work by giving it a grade because this helps students understand that their work is in progress and 'zooms in' on one area to improve. The yellow box focuses students to act on feedback with a clear and specific framework.

The result? You work less. You mark less. You provide specific feedback. The student knows where to work and what to target. Improvements can be identified much more clearly to help aid student progress.

However, yellow boxes are only effective if:

- You allocate time for students to complete them. This could be in class (as an excellent flying start activity – see Section 2, Idea 6, p. 86) or as a specific homework activity, either to complete one particular yellow box or ensure they are all up to date.

- You check students have completed the yellow boxes properly and ensure they redo them if not. Do not accept sloppy or half-hearted work. However, be wary about how many attempts the students need to get things right. 'Mastery requires both the possession of ready knowledge and the conceptual understanding of how to use it.' (Brown et al., 2014) If students do not have the requisite knowledge, you may need to re-teach it.

Finally, the yellow box doesn't have to be yellow – don't get bogged down with the choice of coloured pens!

teacher. I use the question-suggestion-action approach, i.e. the teacher asks, *'Why might XYZ differ from ABC if you increase the amount of 123?'.* The student responds. The teacher then provides a scripted response and a suggested action live in the classroom. Only when a student demonstrates that they have acted on that feedback should the teacher allow the student to move on to the next sequence of the lesson or learning.

'Frequency and speed'

Defined in the EEF report as how often students' work is marked and how quickly the work is returned to the students, these are significant factors in teachers' workload and students' expected levels of progress. Couple this with the demands of working through curriculum reforms and teaching students so they can be successful in their exams, the conflict teachers face every week is clear for anyone to see. Should I ask students to redraft their work? Or should I move on and cover the next part of the curriculum?

Only you can answer these questions but I would suggest considering them after each marking episode and ensuring that you build in regular opportunities for students to recap on work as part of your curriculum plan. 'Spaced learning' or 'spaced practice' is a learning process whereby content is taught repeatedly in short sessions that are broken up by intervals, during which students complete simple, unrelated activities (see Section 2, Idea 4, Evidence, p. 81). A separate report on spaced learning by the EEF, this time with the Centre for Evidence and Social Innovation at Queen's University Belfast, suggests 'teachers and pupils gave substantial positive feedback about the intervention'. A valid question raised in this study, however, is whether it is beneficial to provide less detailed comments quickly or to take the time necessary to provide more thorough feedback (EEF, 2017b).

Well, context is everything, so it is difficult to fully pass comment on the research. However, I do believe that 'less and more often' is the better approach with the recent drive for verbal feedback and research that shows that meaningful feedback delivered in the lesson can make it easier for students to improve. Live-marking permits the teacher to give students concise, regular feedback that can be acted on immediately.

There is a lack of studies in schools on this issue, which suggests that more research would be valuable. You'll be pleased to know that Teacher Toolkit is conducting action research in this area and at the time of writing, we have over 90 sample schools with a potential impact on over 70,000 students. Follow #TTkitResearch for updates.

For me, the one issue stopping verbal live-marking rising through the pile of books stacked on every teacher's desk is having to provide evidence of marking. We cannot evidence verbal feedback as a method of marking for observers who come into lessons to 'look at' progress and attitudes to learning.

If demonstrating evidence is the one reason for marking rather than aiding students' progress, haven't we lost sight of our purpose as teachers?

Live-marking: pros and cons

As we've seen, there are many advantages to live-marking:

- It reduces teachers' workload outside of lesson hours.

- It encourages teachers to give feedback that is diagnostic, closing in on specific areas to improve.

- It allows for a dialogue between teacher and student, enabling the teacher to provide immediate feedback and a suggested action there and then that the student has to act upon before moving on to the next phase of learning.

- It gives students concise, regular feedback, making it easier for them to improve their learning.

However, there are some disadvantages to bear in mind if you try to implement live-marking in your classroom:

- The teacher can only work with one or a small group of students at a time.

- The teacher must monitor the level of detail provided to avoid spending too long with each group.

- Curriculum coverage may suffer if students are spending time in the lesson acting on feedback, especially if redrafting work takes precedence over developing knowledge and skills.

For me, the benefits outweigh the drawbacks and when used well, live-marking enables faster progress over time.

Research into teachers' workload by Peter Sellen for the Education Policy Institute suggests:

- Teachers in England work the longest hours and get paid one of the worst salaries in OECD countries.

- Long working hours are hindering teachers' access to continuing professional development (CPD).

- Long hours, low starting pay and limited access to CPD create a risk of teacher 'burn out', especially in the early stages of careers.

- There is no evidence that additional classroom assistants mean lower working hours for teachers.

- Teachers in 'outstanding' schools (defined by the most recent inspection at the time) tend to work the same number of hours as teachers in other schools, but when compared to 'satisfactory' or 'inadequate' schools, they are less likely to report their workload as 'unmanageable'. (Sellen, 2016)

In May 2016, I watched a TED Talk that changed my working life. In his presentation 'How to Make Work-Life Balance Work', Nigel Marsh, performance coach and bestselling author of *Fat, Forty and Fired*, said we need to redefine our meaning of success, and can't address the issue of workload alone in personal fixes to health and work. We need a cultural shift in attitude. (Marsh, 2010)

CONTINUES OVER PAGE

As an educator, this is a belief I also hold. The moment I watched the video, it reminded me of the 60-hour weeks I was working, failing to spend time with my family. Bogged down in 15 hours of meetings every week and with a never-ending 'to-do list', I made a conscious decision to disconnect. That same day, I removed all the applications on my mobile phone that connected me to work. I promised to time my marking and mark faster, yet more thoughtfully, targeting the work I wanted to assess with students. I resolved to use live-marking and ensure students acted on feedback within a yellow box before allowing them to move forward.

My attitude to work changed and I felt like I was back in control. But, I certainly haven't cracked the workload issue from watching Marsh's video. Taking back control and redefining my version of success in and out of the classroom must become a lifelong habit. And imagine if we all did it – we could reshape the workload landscape, particularly on marking, feedback and assessment, in every school.

We need to redefine what we understand as success. Teacher workload will not improve unless teachers' terms and conditions change to free them from 90% timetable allocations, as this would enable them to mark during the working day. If that's not possible, and it's unlikely given the cuts to education since 2010, with a forecast by the School Teachers Review Body stating there will be further pay constraints, 1% per annum to be exact until 2020 (Wiggins, 2015), marking and teacher workload will never improve. Any solutions will be a fallacy, simply because teachers are not given the time or the pay to do their jobs well enough.

Rebecca Allen, Director of Education Datalab, says, 'there needs to be more radical approaches to cutting teachers' workload'. She suggests outsourcing, which would support written feedback requirements and examination scripts, but could certainly be avoided if the priority of verbal feedback and live-marking was given a higher profile (BBC News, 2015).

Live-marking, like any other workload solution, is a by-product of a broken system, but it offers teachers a temporary classroom strategy that can have a positive impact on learning until the epidemic is fixed.

Marking code

IDEA SNAPSHOT

Ensure your students understand the key assessment points, then develop a simple marking code that works for both you and your students (and is in line with your school policy) to help them understand and respond to your feedback and, ultimately, progress in their learning.

Sharing key assessment points with students is absolutely critical, and this is the first step towards being able to use a simple marking code that students will understand and be able to respond to – and that will save you time.

As Professor John Hattie says, it is important 'for the teacher to communicate the intentions of the lessons and the notions of what success means for these intentions' (Hattie, 2009). Sharing this with students before they start the task you are planning to set them will really help to improve the work they produce and their overall learning. If student work is marked regularly, it means they receive regular feedback, have the opportunity to see how they have performed against the key assessment points and can improve their work with these in mind.

Here are some ways you can ensure your students understand the key assessment points. They will also help your students to assess their own knowledge before a final assessment:

1. An excellent approach is to give students different pieces of work and ask them to rank them and identify the main reasons why one is better than the other. (I've seen this work well in a controlled assessment research project I worked on with Goldsmiths College in 2004, where student coursework was ranked by comparative judgements rather than by an actual checklist.) Once ranked, students should be able to give you the key marking points that make one piece of work better than another. Once this is achieved, the assessment criteria can be provided to lock down understanding.

2. Self-assessment and peer-assessment work wonders. Students grade each other's work and identify the reasons as to why marks are secured or not, helping them to develop an understanding of the key assessment points. This must be done in the right conditions, however. It's impossible to achieve with a difficult class and the climate for learning must be secure. See Section 1, Idea 9, p. 45 for more on self- and peer-assessment.

3. A 'spoof assessment' or a mock exam will help students assess their own performance against the key assessment points. After the assessment, two answers of different quality could be offered for students to assess using the key marking points provided.

Once students understand the key assessment points, you can use a simple marking code to mark students' work against them quickly and effectively.

Teachers must mark for impact, not for frequency, and this is where many marking policies fail. The frequency of marking must be proportionate to curriculum time. There is no specific rule, other than that marking, written or verbal, should be regular. This is a common-sense approach for schools to adopt across the board. Ensuring that marking is proportionate ensures equality between departments who see their classes for one lesson a week compared with other teachers, perhaps in different subject areas, who see students more often. I teach more classes in design technology and art, but I may see the students in those classes less often when compared to an English teacher, who may see the same students in a lesson five or six times a week. Whichever way you look at it, it is essential to provide regular feedback that has a rapid turnaround time and encourages students to engage with it and use it to improve their learning.

This is where a simple marking code can help. It will:

- speed up your marking, ensuring you can feed back to students more regularly and more quickly

- enable students to engage with your feedback quickly and easily so they can see how they have fared against the key assessment points and what they need to do to improve their performance.

Developing a marking code

I've developed so many marking codes over the past decade. Some have been awful and rarely used, while others were too cumbersome for teachers to understand, never mind the students! What works best is simplicity and clear symbols that have stood the test of time.

A quick note, though: while marking codes are typically very helpful, you should make sure you are still in line with your school's marking policy. If teachers create their own marking code without taking school policy into consideration, they are generating further discrepancies and inconsistencies between classrooms, which can lead to students becoming confused.

The following is a typical – and simple and sensible – marking code. For me, the first five symbols would be what I'd want for the perfect set of symbols to use when providing written feedback on a student's work.

Symbol	Meaning
✓	Correct/good point/well written (in more practical subjects, such as PE, this could be a 'thumbs-up').
X	Incorrect/wrong point (in more practical subjects, such as PE, this could be a 'thumbs-down').
Sp	Correct a spelling mistake (these words should be written in a spelling log).
?	This does not make sense/the handwriting or sentence needs to be clearer.
∧	You need to add a word.
//	You need to start a new paragraph.
e.g.	Provide examples.

NOTE: If schools want to adopt a growth mindset approach (see Section 1, Idea 2, p. 13), they could replace **X** (wrong) with a ½ or a 'sideways thumb'.

I don't believe there is much need for anything else. Anything more and it becomes confusing and will make any marking code too difficult to use and, worse, too complicated for students and parents to understand.

So, what's missing for you? Or is there anything in the above that is irrelevant for your students to progress? Is there anything you could live without? Scribble your ideas for a perfect marking code for your classroom in the table below and share a photo with me on Twitter at #MarkPlanTeach.

The simplest marking code in the world

Symbol	Meaning

EVIDENCE

Fascinating research from the Department for Education (DfE, 2016) highlighted three simple words that best summed up useful marking, feedback and assessment:

- 'Meaningful'
- 'Manageable'
- 'Motivating'

The research conducted was extensive and involved a varied selection of educationalists who reported on 'working to remove unnecessary workload for teachers'. Let's look at exactly what the DfE means by each of these words.

'Meaningful'

According to the DfE, 'meaningful' marking will depend on the age group of your students, the subject you are teaching and the particular piece of work you are marking. They suggest that teachers adapt their approach according to the needs of their students and 'incorporate the outcomes into subsequent planning and teaching'.

For me, 'meaningful' marking basically means that it has to work and have demonstrable outcomes for you and your students. When students know the key assessment points, a simple, understandable marking code will help with this. Try using your marking code alongside the yellow box approach (see Section 1, Idea 3, p. 17) to reduce your workload even further and zoom in on feedback areas for improvement. But remember that 'meaningful' feedback can also be verbal and does not require evidencing for the 'marking police'.

'Manageable'

The DfE argues that the amount of marking a teacher does should be proportionate to the outcomes that it has for teachers and students, and schools should develop assessment policies that take into account 'the cost and time-effectiveness of marking in relation to the overall workload of teachers'.

I agree that this should be written into assessment policy, but I believe it should be guidance. Perhaps half the problem with teachers' workload is that we do not guide one another. Instead, we place unnecessary themes into school policy to hold good teachers to account. A marking policy is not statutory. It is something created by school leaders to support consistency. The danger is it becomes something to beat teachers over the head with and leads to *unmanageable* workloads. Quite the opposite to the advice from the DfE research.

So, how do we measure the costs of this workload?

Simple sums will tell you that a secondary teacher working a full-time timetable, with 15 different classes and 20-30 students in each, will have to mark the work of 450 students. With one period of a 25-period timetable costing the equivalent of £2,000 per academic year, teachers are supposed to spend 10% of their time on planning and assessment. That's two hours per week and equates to 76 hours during a 38-week academic year, or the equivalent, for every classroom teacher to use wisely throughout the year. If we take those original 450 students and divide this by 76 hours, that is the equivalent of 16 minutes per student per year! We can already see this is a huge and unrealistic expectation and costing a teacher's timetable is equally unhelpful.

Something has to change and keeping marking codes as simple as possible, with the onus on the student to understand the key assessment points and act on feedback, is a good starting point.

'Motivating'

The DfE advocates marking that helps 'motivate students to progress' but acknowledges that 'sometimes short, challenging comments or oral feedback are more effective' here than 'in-depth' and 'universally positive' comments. The DfE also argues that a teacher 'doing more work than their students [...] can become a disincentive for students to accept challenges and take responsibility for improving their work'.

How you motivate your students when giving them feedback is best left to you. You know your students better than I do, and we all know that students and their moods are often unpredictable. What they like one day might not be what they like another.

Nevertheless, 'motivating' marking should help to engage students to make progress. 'Meaningful' and 'manageable' are key here. Brief yet challenging marking that students can understand, such as a simple marking code, makes sure that the person receiving the feedback will complete more actions than the person providing it. This is more motivating for the student *and* the teacher. If not followed, we end up in a downward spiral where sanctions to complete work outweigh anything positive going on in the classroom.

 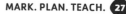

Psychology and...
feedback

Feedback is a process and not a one-off event. Psychologically, whether you intend it or not, when offering feedback you will be engaging with a student's sense of self as a person and as a learner. Feedback is self-related, often in terms of self-development, and as a consequence, I recommend that feedback should be both motivational and developmental in nature. It should motivate a student to believe that they can make progress and do better. This is often achieved by reminding them of what they have already achieved – in terms of learning outcomes but also in terms of cognitive and emotional processes associated with learning. Feedback has to be developmental by providing clarity about next steps for action. Feedback should result in action. It is important to check the meaning that a student makes from your feedback: has the student understood, in exact terms, what the next steps are and what success will look like?

Feedback is also language dependent and relationship dependent. When giving feedback, teacher language becomes particularly important. You have to think carefully about the language that you use, as what you say is open to being processed differently by different individuals in different contexts. I suggest avoiding the phrase, 'I like it *but*…'. One of the reasons is that once a student hears the word 'but', they may disregard what you have said before the word 'but' – sometimes at an unconscious level – and only focus on what comes afterwards. This can result in the student assuming that you do not actually like their work at all, which was not your feedback intention. Instead, you could say, 'I like it *and*…'.

Firstly, this emphasises and validates what you like. The word 'and' is non-judgemental; it is not processed as dismissive. It also creates a better psychological space from which to engage the student in a discussion about what they think they could have done differently or additionally. There is a huge difference between how 'I like it *but*…' and how 'I like it *and*…' are psychologically processed, especially in terms of the emotional responses and behaviours they can elicit.

Relationships have a fundamental impact on how feedback is given and received and on whether it results in positive or negative outcomes. It is easier to receive feedback when you feel that the person giving it respects you and that it is being given with best intentions and your needs at the forefront. I believe there is one principle that should apply to feedback in all of its guises: feedback should be given for the benefit of the receiver and not for the benefit of the giver.

– Dr Tim O'Brien

Celebrate mistakes!

IDEA SNAPSHOT

Making mistakes is important. It helps us to learn new things, builds our confidence and encourages us to take risks. How can we use marking and feedback to help students not only learn from their mistakes but also to understand the value of making them?

John Wooden, an American basketball coach, once said:

> 'If you're not making mistakes, you're not doing anything. I'm positive a doer makes mistakes.'

I, too, am a strong believer in the importance of making mistakes. Let's look at it from the perspective of my own career as a teacher. For the past 25 years, I've been teaching in the classroom in some capacity (as a deputy headteacher, I still teach but not as much as before) and I believe making mistakes and, more importantly, reflecting on them has made me a better teacher.

The expertise of a head of department and a good scheme of work were everything I needed as a new teacher, but making mistakes and reflecting on them over the three decades I have been in the classroom has placed me in a good position and improved my practice. All good teachers – whether teaching ten or twenty hours per week – need to be able to reflect on their personal journey in the classroom. They must have the capacity to consider what works and what interventions are needed to reach a student, whether disadvantaged, gifted or challenging. This was instilled in me early on during teacher training at university, but it took me some time to put it into practice.

As my experience developed, I taught more lessons, took more risks and made more mistakes. But, crucially, at the end of both brilliant lessons and disastrously epic failures, I had learnt to reflect. Many nights I would go home and question what I was doing. I was constantly tweaking my teaching, only to have it all shoved in my face the very next lesson. You see, in teaching, riding a bicycle is very much the same as working in the classroom. Some days it works as expected but on other days, parts need tightening and a little tinkering is required to maintain your performance. If you do not oil the chain or the wheels, the bike moves more slowly and starts to squeak and crank as the pedals push slowly around the same cycle. The academic year is very much the same – it peaks and troughs at various points throughout the year, then repeats all over again.

I may not teach as much as I used to – or ride a bike for that matter – but I wouldn't be the teacher I am today if I hadn't made mistakes or tweaked my practice along the way or, even more importantly, hadn't been encouraged to take risks in a school where trust was given to me as a classroom teacher, a middle leader, then as a senior leader. I was confident that colleagues walking past or into my classroom were not assessing the quality of what I was doing from a thirty-second or twenty-minute observation, regardless of eyeballs and hands flicking through books with majestic grandeur. This was not the climate in which I worked and I hope it is not the one in which you work either.

Teachers make mistakes. So do students and so do school leaders. Yet, these mistakes are mostly miniscule and easy to fix in the classroom. It's fine to make as many of them as you can, as long as you don't repeat the same cataclysmic errors time and time again. And we've all witnessed those…

To lose our fear of failure, however, requires practice. We might say that cycling up and down hills – namely teaching tough lessons and classes where relationships have taken months to form – requires a high level of self-esteem before we are confident enough to take risks in the classroom. If confidence is not fostered in our formative years, it will be much more difficult to break old habits in our latter years, perhaps making us less likely to take risks and learn from our mistakes. Dr Tim O'Brien argues that we should be thinking about self-esteems instead of self-esteem, as this changes our own emotional landscape and is critical to our confidence and wellbeing (O'Brien, 2015). He has more to say about this later in the book.

Encouraging students to learn from mistakes

So, how do we instil this confidence and ability to learn from mistakes into our students in time for them to become self-assured, risk-taking learners and eventually adults?

The answer goes back to the importance of diagnostic feedback and building a growth mindset. We looked at the 'not yet' strategy in Idea 2 of this section, which could certainly be used to help students understand the benefits of making mistakes, but let's consider here a few more helpful marking strategies that will enable your students to lose their fear of failure.

Delayed marking

In this technique, no grade or score is given on the work (although the teacher can record a grade in their private written or online records). Written comments from the teacher address the quality of the work in terms of the assessment criteria and give guidance as to how to improve. Students are given time to read the comments in class. After some time (e.g. one week), the teacher talks with students individually to discuss the work, the feedback, any improvements required and finally the grade or mark that was given to it.

Delayed marking helps students to focus on the feedback and how to act upon it, rather than simply being demotivated and demoralised by a grade or a score. When discussing the piece of work with each individual student, you can check they have understood what they need to do to improve and make this feel manageable and achievable.

Re-marking

This involves asking students to redo a piece of work for you after a lesson, focusing on how to improve it. Only accept the work if their improvements mean they would score a higher mark because they understand your feedback and have acted on it. This may be difficult to ascertain without actually marking the work, but a check to see if improvements are clear in relation to the original feedback should always be super quick to determine.

Similarly to delayed marking, your (hopefully positive!) comments on the students' second drafts will prove to them that it is possible to learn from mistakes and will encourage them to see the value of considering and acting upon feedback.

Responding to marking

This technique is similar to re-marking. You provide students with written feedback on their work and then ask students to redraft it based on your comments. The students should then write an appropriate response to the feedback, ideally signposting where to find any redrafting. The redrafted piece of work should **not** be marked until the student has responded.

The danger of re-marking in both of these techniques, however, is that it increases workload. We should be very careful about when we ask for redrafted work. It should be a carefully selected activity and we should make sure it is for improvement, not evidence for an observer. Also, to reduce workload when you do re-mark, you could try targeting only one area of the work for assessment by using the yellow box methodology. See Section 1, Idea 3, p. 17 for more details.

Mastery marking

Mastery marking is the practice of only accepting a piece of work when it is of a specific quality. For example, ask students to continue to redraft and resubmit their work as many times as it takes for them to achieve an 'A' grade.

With the promise of an 'A' grade on the horizon, this strategy will not only enable students to practise learning from their mistakes independently, but also instil in them a sense of determination to produce the best piece of work they possibly can.

Plus, minus, equals (+, –, =)

Mark student work in relation to previous work, but this time only using your simple marking code (see Section 1, Idea 4, p. 23) or even better, only plus, minus or equals signs to indicate whether the quality of the work has improved and whether the marks would be higher or lower. For example:

- if the most recent piece of work is of the same quality as the last, it receives a '=';

- if it is better than the last, it receives a '+';

- if it is not as good as the last, it receives a '–'.

Hopefully, the redrafted work will be full of '+' signs, proving to your students the value of learning from mistakes. However, by using only a simple code of symbols, this technique puts the impetus on the student to look back at the changes they made in their second draft and understand why these had a positive or negative impact on the quality of their work. It will show them *how well* they have learned from their mistakes and help them build this skill even further.

These strategies will ensure your students understand that making mistakes and redrafting are part of the learning process and nothing at all to worry about. This will encourage students to take risks in an attempt to push their work to the next level of attainment, raising their self-esteem and confidence, and helping them to make progress in their learning.

Psychology and...
making mistakes

Learning involves forgetting and can be dependent upon remembering what you have forgotten. Learning also involves making mistakes and can be dependent upon how those mistakes inform new learning. Way back in 1978, Donald Norman proposed a tentative model of complex learning. This model focuses solely on the cognitive aspects of learning. Four cognitive stages were proposed:

1. **Accretion**: an organic process whereby new information is processed through multisensory channels. (It is worth noting that at this early point in the learning process, people can already experience cognitive, emotional and sensory overload.)

2. **Restructuring**: we begin to think about, make meaning out of and then act upon information. Accumulation becomes less prominent.

3. **Tuning in**: we 'get it'. The penny drops. Learning becomes meaningful to the learner.

4. **Automisation**: learning is now known. It becomes familiar and automatic. The learner is more independent.

Automisation and independence enable us to, for example, play with knowledge. However, learning can also become less familiar and increasingly unrequired and at this point, we no longer retain it; we forget what has been learned. This is one model, one way of looking at learning. I highlight this model here because when you consider it, you can see that there are stages – as well as transitions and connections between stages – where mistakes will inevitably be made. Learning is a challenge and making mistakes is an essential part of the learning process. I also include it because I assume that you might not be aware of the model. Therefore in understanding the model, you have to engage with the processes that are described within the model itself.

During the learning process, cognition and emotion engage in a complex dance. When we are learning, especially something new, we send out a party invitation to our emotions. Confidence might arrive for one student, anxiety for another. Anxiety can generalise and free-float in an unresolved manner but, given the opportunity, it can also arrive at breakneck speed and locate itself in the learning process. This can encourage some students to doubt their potential to succeed and entice them to do whatever it takes to disengage from learning. One of the tasks of a teacher is to help students to understand that it is possible to embrace mistakes and learn from them.

In 2009, Hattie highlighted the value of developing an environment in schools where mistakes are valued as an essential part of learning (Hattie, 2009). Of course, teachers can benefit from a culture where they are given permission to embrace their own mistakes too.

– Dr Tim O'Brien

Mind the gaps!

IDEA SNAPSHOT

Re-teaching is a necessary part of any scheme of work if there is an important element of the module, topic or lesson that students just haven't grasped. Don't worry! It happens to all teachers, but the important thing is to spot the 'gap' in your students' learning through marking and assessment and then go back and address it again. I rarely see this happen unless it is for revision purposes, but how and when you do this is critical.

Psychologist Hermann Ebbinghaus, famous for his research on memory, related forgetting to the passage of time in his 'forgetting curve'. The curve shows that information is lost over time if no attempt is made to retain it (Ebbinghaus, 1885). Of course, a lot more research on memory has been conducted since, with many arguing that there are other factors that affect how quickly we forget information, including the nature of that information and its significance to us. Nevertheless, Ebbinghaus' premise that information is forgotten over time if we do not review it in the days after we learn it is one that many still stand by today and that we, as teachers, see happening before our very eyes (much more often than we would like!).

Re-teaching is therefore crucial, but we must understand what, when, how and why we can re-teach to best effect so we can fit it into our jam-packed curriculums. This is where marking and feedback techniques, such as focused marking, can help.

Focused marking

Focused marking involves marking students' work against one or two specific criteria, which reflect the key aspects of learning that the teacher wants their students to grasp. There may in fact be many different criteria that could be considered, but this technique allows the teacher to provide more focused and detailed feedback that relates to the most important learning points. The teacher's markbook contains the two aspects of learning being marked, rather than the title of the work set, the grade or the total number of marks available. Often, by breaking the marking down in this way, the teacher can spot the gaps in the learning of both an individual student and the class as a whole. This is an excellent strategy to deploy when marking mock examination papers.

Closing the gap

So, how do we then go on to close any gaps we have identified? How can we help students find the desired knowledge in applying the skills to master the curriculum? Perhaps we can find a quicker way to progress, rather than following a traditional teaching sequence. This would ensure curriculum coverage with enough slack to re-teach gaps in learning to individuals or the entire class when needed.

When I think about some of the best teaching that I have observed, I can extract a clear commonality. No matter how high the standards of assessment or how quickly the students needed to grasp a concept, there was always an explicit model provided and it was a step that *could not* be missed. Sometimes, a direct instruction or modelling in class opened the teaching sequence; sometimes the students had to experiment and investigate that perfect solution. Regardless, the students were *always* clear about what it was they were trying to achieve and what that could look like.

This direct, explicit form of teaching isn't a one-size-fits-all approach. Rather, it is about providing the right level of scaffold, support and inspiration for your students. When done correctly, it can allow you enough time in class to re-teach the aspects of the curriculum that your students are struggling to master.

Here are my top ten tips for using modelling to support students to help reduce gaps in learning:

1. Show what a good piece of work looks like, and how it is created, step by step, piece by piece. Demonstrate the whole process of creation, whether that is the perfect cartwheel, a neatly crafted butt-joint or a well-written argument.

2. Talk it through, and not only the things you decide to do, but also the things that you don't. The class need to hear you say, 'I know it can't be 17 because the answer's final digit is 0' or 'I need to say "sat" but I want it to show that I'm grumpy. I'll use "slouched"'.

3. Speak your thoughts. It is the very thoughts that our students cannot hear or see that they need to understand the most – those times of doubt and uncertainty when you question your knowledge base; the conundrums of which method would be best or which style of recording is most suitable; or those penny-dropping moments when the connections between ideas finally make sense.

4. Make mistakes! One of the hardest skills in the world is editing, especially when you're not yet wise or good enough. Work needs to be modelled. Students need to see that crossing out and making mistakes are part of the learning process and nothing to panic about. See Section 1, Idea 5, p. 29 for more on this.

5. Show students what to do when you don't know what to do. Model 'just drawing a line' when you are not sure of the word to put and don't want to waste ten minutes' thinking time. Demonstrate 'just having a go' at a problem when you don't know where to start. Talk through any doubts you have and how you sometimes just need to try to see what happens.

6. Don't use up all of your modelling tips at the beginning of a lesson. It can be equally (and sometimes more) valuable to stop the class after an initial experiment to address any common misconceptions found, or at the end of the lesson to build success criteria together and challenge thinking.

7. In a classroom climate built on trust and a belief that with good practice you can get better, a visualiser is your friend and a piece of work can be the next top model.

8. Never make assumptions about what the students already know and understand. Never. The most basic things also need modelling – from letter formation and counting slowly to 'what does good listening look like?'.

9. Model the learning in many ways – as imaginatively as possible. It is important that your modelling acts as a creative catalyst and not as an inhibitor, especially for the most inspired in your classroom. They need to see possibilities, not one solution.

10. Have at the forefront of your mind your goal – and within this should be the independent application of whatever it is you are teaching! Some students will be ready to run and make it entirely their own after one tiny exposure. Some may need a little guided work, some may need a confidence boost and some may need the same skill modelled in different contexts many, many times before those connections are forged. Only you will know what works for your students more than any other. A secure overview is essential (see Section 1, Idea 1, p. 6).

Use your marking to identify the gaps in your students' learning and put these modelling tips into practice to close the gaps and provide your students with quality first teaching (see more on this in Section 2, Idea 7, p. 91).

CLOSE THE GAP

Psychology and....
confidence

I would like to reflect on what Ross has said about learning gaps and the need for some students to have a 'confidence boost' to bridge these gaps. There is a fascinating and complex psychological space where teaching transforms into learning. Learning gaps can occur at various places in that space.

If a student spends too long in a learning gap, it rapidly starts to feel like a confidence-collapsing chasm. To boost someone's confidence, you have to know what you are trying to boost. Confidence begins inside your head. When it begins, it is invisible but it does not stay that way. We can see and feel confidence or lack of confidence in the way that people behave. To feel more confident and be more confident, you have to trust yourself and believe in yourself. You have to believe you can do it, trust yourself to step out of your comfort zone, take a leap of faith and then have a go and do it. Creating an environment where people are encouraged to have a go, whilst remembering the value of mistakes, is essential to promote learning. I must emphasise that being confident is not about flooding your mind with positive thoughts and denying the existence of negative thoughts. That is an illusory path to gaining or boosting confidence. To be more confident, you have to acknowledge negative thoughts and emotions so that you can process and deal with them.

Sometimes, the barriers to confidence are inside your head, but they can also exist outside of your head too. The same applies to confidence enablers. If a student needs a confidence boost to help them to overcome a learning gap, explore with them where, why and how the gap might be happening. This helps them to learn about learning. For example, if an emotional factor is relevant, you can encourage the student to identify and name the emotion or emotions that might be holding them back. As a teacher, in your mind, amplify the learning gap, dive in and take a forensic rummage around so that you can see what it is that is creating a barrier to learning for a student. You may have to mind the gap but you also have to find the gap. Think in terms of the ecology of teaching and learning, and avoid assuming that a learning gap is inevitably due to a deficit within the student. Barriers to learning do not only occur inside someone's head, they can also occur outside of someone's head too.

– Dr Tim O'Brien

Find and fix

IDEA 7

IDEA SNAPSHOT

Although it's important for teachers to identify gaps in their students' learning, it is crucial that we also encourage students to be independent in identifying problems with their own work and areas of the curriculum where they need support. A good strategy is to give students time in class to 'find and fix' their mistakes.

As highlighted in my **5 Minute Marking Plan** (see Section 1, Idea 1, p. 6), once a teacher has spent time adding comments to a student's piece of work, the student should go back and either correct errors or redo parts of their work that need improvement. This is not required for every piece of work but it should be a regular exercise to help students learn from their mistakes, develop a growth mindset and ultimately deepen their learning and understanding.

In previous ideas, we've looked at ways in which teachers can identify areas for improvement and encourage their students to correct and redraft their work. However, it is also important that we give students the opportunity to reflect on their work independently and think about where they have met assessment criteria and where they might need to improve.

This is a key part of the learning process. It helps your students to identify gaps in their own knowledge so they can improve their own understanding independently or seek support from you. Think about it: every student developing their own personalised action plan. They will be completely in control of their learning. Think about how this will increase their motivation. All the teacher needs to do is to identify which student needs to act on what and when.

So, how can teachers develop a reliable method to help students reflect on their work and build an action plan for their learning? Well, this is an interesting question, which will have countless permutations for different subjects, topics and styles of teaching, but allow me to offer five suggestions that will be timeless in the vast majority of classrooms.

Find and fix

The best strategy to help students reflect on their own work is to give them time to correct and redo their work during lessons. This can be a mixture of quick fixes and a deeper redraft to demonstrate that work meets assessment standards. To take this further, don't mark answers as correct or incorrect but simply tell students the number of answers that are wrong. Ask them to 'find and fix' their mistakes either individually or in groups.

Student marking (self- and peer-assessment)

Ask students to mark their own work and that of their peers using a student-friendly marking scheme. See Section 1, Idea 9, p. 45 for more on this.

Colouring in

Give students coloured pens and ask them to highlight on their work where they have shown evidence of different skills according to the requirements of the mark scheme. This allows students to reflect on their own learning but also shows you whether they understand what is required of them according to the assessment framework or if this is something you need to revisit with one specific student or your class as a whole.

Traffic lights

Ask students to leave red, amber and green coloured dots on their work to indicate areas where they have struggled and areas where they think they have done well. This targets the assessment for the students and the teacher on the areas that need it most. The colour ratings work as follows:

- **Red** indicates areas where the student has struggled, still does not understand or needs further support.
- **Amber** indicates that further work is needed to secure meaningful understanding.
- **Green** indicates that the work is meeting assessment criteria.

The beauty of this process is that students are highlighting to the teacher what *they* don't understand. The teacher can then look over the work, check whether they agree with the students' coloured dots and even give an overall red, amber or green mark for the piece of work. The teacher then gives the student further support and guidance in any areas marked with red or amber dots and the student redrafts them in an attempt to achieve a green dot. The final assessment can be calculated from the number of green comments actioned against the assessment criteria.

Crack this one and student confidence soars, as does their motivation!

Aim for the next level

Students compare their work to exemplars that are at the next level of achievement. The students identify where they can improve their work in order to emulate these exemplars. They realise that they need to set themselves higher standards and find that it is possible to improve what they thought was already a good piece of work. It also makes the next level feel more attainable, particularly when the example has been completed by a peer.

Psychology and... motivation

It is tempting to think of motivation as being about our motives but it is far more helpful to think of motivation as being about motion: the desire to move from A to B. Inside our heads, we can be motivated to pull ourselves away from some situations – often for physical and emotional protection – and push ourselves towards others.

Learning involves challenges and students are expected to rise to such challenges. To be motivated to set about rising to a challenge, we have to be willing to accept that success does not happen in a straight line. The road to success contains bumpy terrain – it can involve unpredictable twists and turns and there is always the potential for setbacks along the way. This is one of the reasons why resilience is an important factor in achieving consistent motivation. Some students have a secure emotional base from which to rise to such challenges. Others, for a variety of reasons including, for example, the effects of emotional or developmental trauma, difficulties related to self-regulation or the rumbling presence of self-limiting beliefs, will need support in helping them to be convinced that they really can navigate the road ahead. This can even apply to taking the smallest steps on a learning journey.

Our feelings can be a predictor of the nature and duration of our motivation. A student can feel energised and inquisitive but they can also feel anxious and disheartened; feelings affect motivation and behaviour in differing ways. Internal motivation can be influenced positively or negatively by external factors too. The degree of autonomy that a person is afforded, or perceives that they are afforded, informs their sense of self-control and self-determination and will influence motivation. The sense of meaning or purpose a person attaches to the activities and tasks they are engaged in will inevitably influence their motivation.

There are many available perspectives and theories that aim to offer explanatory insight into what motivation is and why it might result in specific types of behaviours and outcomes. For example, biological needs, such as the need to survive, might motivate us to behave in particular ways, whereas psychological needs, such as the desire to be the best we can be, might cause us to behave differently. However, whether they are biological, psychological or social, our needs are interrelated and they will impact upon each other.

– Dr Tim O'Brien

'Fishing without the bait'

IDEA SNAPSHOT

Moderating student work as an individual teacher, a department or as an entire school is important for lesson and curriculum planning and assessing attitudes to learning and progress over a period of time. However, it should be a meaningful process for the student, the teacher and the school in question. To use a phrase coined by Pam Fearnley, School Improvement Consultant and ex-HMI (pamb566@btinternet.com), we should never go 'fishing without the bait'; we should always take context into account.

When teaching, it is useful to ask yourself if there is a gap between the learning you *wanted* to happen and the learning that *actually* happened. This can be evaluated in the lesson through questioning and student participation, but it is often after the lesson – when looking at the work completed – that a teacher can really see what learning has (or has not) taken place. There is often a large disparity between teacher delivery and outcome.

Instead of spending hours marking every single piece of student work in detail, you could use your marking time to moderate and review the work your students have produced, compare it to previous work and ascertain what your students have learnt. This will show you what needs to be changed in a scheme of work and what classroom activity you could try with your students next.

You should also regularly moderate and review student work with colleagues either in your department or in other parts of the school, so you can all look at work from students in classes other than your own. This is a powerful way to improve the teaching programme and would be a useful departmental or whole-school professional development activity if schemes of work require updating or reform. It is vital to build frequent moderation into curriculum planning and assessment as a teacher or a department moves through a scheme of work with the students. It will also tell you whether a student is working better in someone else's subject and it may even give you some ideas of how you could teach or motivate that student more effectively in your own lessons.

Work sampling

Now, this is one to discuss with your school leadership team. There has been much discussion that work sampling – namely observers looking in students' exercise books to moderate quality of marking, assessment and teaching – has replaced the frenzy of grading individual lessons and having observers determine the quality of teaching. There has also been a call for evidence to validate how reliable work sampling can be to judge quality of teaching.

I would support the need for evidence in this area but for too long, schools have either conducted or been on the receiving end of work sampling *without* context. As Pam Fearnley would say, observers have been 'fishing without the bait'. They look in students' books at random without any context. The classes, students and teachers are not pre-determined. There are no conversations. No data is used and the process is very much a tick-box exercise.

We are all guilty of this – even me! As author Seth Godin said in 2012, 'Sometimes we can't measure what we need, so we invent a proxy; something easier to measure'. Work sampling is often left to ad-hoc procedures that lead to ad-hoc judgements and conclusions. For example, an observer arrives in your classroom, sits down quietly at the back where there is an empty seat and proceeds to flick through the book of Student A and Student B who are sitting next to them. Then, an assumption is made of the outcomes from what is seen or not seen.

Consider the classroom next door. Same project, same age group and similar ability, but students are working with a different teacher. For the sake of an easy argument, let's just assume both teachers are very similar in manner, style and performance. Another observer completes the same exercise. They arrive in the classroom, sit down quietly at the back where there is an empty seat and proceed to flick through the book of Student A and Student B. Only this time, Student B is absent and the work of Student C is sampled. Student A has lost their book and started a new exercise book last month. This explains why there is no work, but the observer – too busy and miffed that they are having to sample work in their free lesson because someone else is chasing their paperwork too – does not ask the student why the work is missing. There is no context, no conversation with the student or the teacher. Immediately, we are making a dangerously weak process even more unreliable.

However, all is not lost. I do believe work sampling is critical to the life of a school to help assess attitudes to learning and progress over a period of time, but only when completed in reliable conditions.

So what's the solution?

Well, first of all, it is critical that work sampling is conducted in the right conditions, with the input (purpose) and output (outcomes) communicated before, during and after the process. More importantly, the teacher of the student whose work is being sampled must be involved. An observer should never pick students at random for work sampling. They should instead select a range of students based on their prior data or starting points (for example, their Key Stage 2 results) and use this information to assess progress over time. It would be recommended to select a range of students, including high-, middle- and low-attaining students, students from disadvantaged backgrounds (or Pupil Premium students in England) and SEND, G&T and EAL students.

The observer should then:

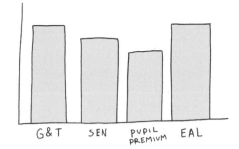

1. Look at pieces of work by the targeted group of students, keeping in mind that this is *just one source of evidence* and that every book and every student has a story to tell.

2. Have a face-to-face conversation with the classroom teacher, so they can share information about the child and make observers aware of other factors that are not clear from the students' exercise books, such as absence.

3. Interview the students themselves.

When we have 'the bait' (the context), exercise books can show:

*   teacher expectations

*   classroom routines

*   access to the curriculum

*   use of the school's marking code

*   attitudes to learning (i.e. if students take pride in their work; look for graffiti or ripped pages)

*   the quality of written feedback

*   if effort is recognised (i.e. if students are proud of their achievements)

*   if students are acting on feedback

*   if students are making expected progress.

Note that this process would need to be adapted for practical subjects where performance in plays, sports and music, for example, could be observed in application of knowledge and verbal feedback. Again, this is something the observer would have to complete in the lesson itself with the teacher and the students. The process should not penalise teachers and students simply because of the nature of the subject matter. It should be flexible, but also fair and robust.

I do confess, though, that more work needs to be done to eradicate schools using work sampling as a procedure for judging individual teachers. A one-size-fits-all, binary 'marking compliance' is applied in many schools. Little evidence of red and green pen in a student's book and the teacher is still likely to be viewed as underperforming, a maverick, lazy or non-compliant.

Much more research is needed to find out what evaluation system works best, what methodology leads to reliable assessments about the quality of teaching and if work sampling is a meaningful process for the student, the teacher or just the observer. If it's the latter in your school, then it's about time we all started to change the dialogue of work sampling for the benefit of teachers and students.

EVIDENCE

If you look at sources of research into assessment, particularly comparative research, it is clear that the reliability of marking is flawed when work is marked in different subject areas. In a study by R. J. L. Murphy, eight GCE examinations in a variety of subject areas were compared for marking reliability. The results showed that subject area, the number of questions on the paper and the type of questions asked all had an effect on the reliability of marking in these examinations (Murphy, 1978).

On Google Scholar, there are over 315,000 entries for 'marking reliability'. It makes me wonder if marking in the classroom, and not just in public examinations or in studies conducted in a university environment, is equally unreliable. How often have you moderated work with colleagues in your department, only to find one of you is wildly off the mark? I'm sure we all have, and there are countless hours of work here that are not captured by research, case studies or data.

So, there are discrepancies between what teachers, even in the same school, are doing in their classrooms and when marking on their kitchen tables. And there could be a million and one reasons for this too: time, accountability, type of assessment, distractions, workload, and whether the work is high stakes or not. I would not mark a piece of homework as seriously as I would a mock examination, and there would be good reason for that, but lack of importance when assessing a piece of work would definitely lead to greater unreliability.

This means that moderation is essential, whether as a department, a whole school or more broadly. However, teachers are not very comfortable with being judged by another professional, largely because of what it can do to your confidence and worse, your career. It is therefore necessary that if we, as a profession, are to use students' work as a measure of teaching and student performance, we need to improve our methodology for doing so.

Sandra Johnson's article, 'On the Reliability of High-Stakes Teacher Assessment', supports this (Johnson, 2013). She observes that 'increasing reliance is being placed on teacher assessment in high-stakes contexts in many countries around the world'. We know that teacher assessment has a place in our schools and classrooms, but as Johnson asks, 'what is the evidence regarding the reliability of teacher assessment in high-stakes contexts?'. I would ask the same question on behalf of all teachers, whether in low- or high-stakes assessment.

Johnson suggests that 'the evidence is limited and often ambiguous' and research shows that teachers are influenced by 'factors such as gender, socio-economic background, effort and behaviour' and this can cause bias in their marking. Is it any wonder then that our assessment framework has been overhauled in England? If work requires a degree of subjectivity – which teaching obviously does – then there will always be variation. So it is not a matter of scrapping assessment all together, but more about questioning how we can improve assessment and marking, so they are more reliable for all of us, including the child who has to live with the grade.

Smarter not harder

IDEA SNAPSHOT

Introduce self-assessment and peer-assessment into your marking routine to ensure your students are working harder than you are! Take some time at the beginning of term to teach them how to do this effectively and you will reduce your workload and make your marking smarter for the rest of the year.

As Nigel Marsh, performance coach and bestselling author of *Fat, Forty and Fired*, says, 'If you do not define your own work-life balance, your employer will' (Marsh, 2010). Students should be working harder than the teacher. Of course, this all *sounds* great and I'm well aware that I might be making even the hardiest teacher's blood boil by saying this. So how can we all achieve the impossible? Thirty sweaty students pushing pen to paper faster than Usain Bolt reaching the end of a 100-metre sprint!

Teachers like to maintain high expectations and it's all too easy to be snowed under with workload, but we must be flexible, not just in the classroom but with our own workload and wellbeing. To do this, it is vital that schools reduce the quantity of checklists and encourage staff to work smarter, not harder. This can also be achieved by individual teachers in the classroom, but it is not possible without taking something away so we can replace it with something new.

Teachers should not only be defined by student outcomes, which is our current problem in education. If education is to make any progress with teacher work-life balance, we need a serious debate. Success in education cannot be defined by examination results alone and the sooner we realise this at government level, the sooner we will start to rescue teachers who are reaching unprecedented burnout levels.

To have mastered a skill or concept, a student must possess a deep understanding and be capable of applying that skill or concept creatively and in a range of different contexts. Therefore, a good teacher does not work harder; they work more effectively to ensure a deep understanding is developed. To achieve this, it is not how hard or how many hours teachers work in and out of school; they simply work smarter and more effectively to ensure a greater impact on students. I know, I know. There I go again and you're about to throw this book against a brick wall or bash it across another colleague's head! What you want to know is how can I work smarter when...

- My line manager has told me to mark this way.

- Our school policy says…

- The Grim Reaper is due any day!

- Our leadership team are conducting a work sample next week. I must mark, mark, mark…

- [Student name] has asked me to mark their work tonight and I can't let them down.

- A parent has just emailed me and they want a reply before they arrive at reception in the morning!

- I'm leading department moderation this week. I must take an exemplar set of class books to show off!

- I teach 450 students every week.

- [Any other reasonable excuse.]

One strategy I suggest trying out to work smarter, reduce your workload and ensure your students are putting in more effort than you is implementing a system of self-assessment and peer-assessment in your classroom.

The importance of self-assessment and peer-assessment

Self-assessment and peer-assessment are not simply tools we may choose to use but are the foundation of the reconceptualisation of the roles of the teacher and student and the entire process of education.

As we saw in Section 1, Idea 1, p. 6, all assessments should be related to the curriculum that is being taught in the school. Most schools in the UK will have started the process of developing a revised assessment framework in line with the curriculum reforms that have taken place or will have adopted one that has been created externally. Those readers who are finding that this process of change is still the order of the day will know that it requires time-consuming, ongoing evaluation and adjustments.

Nevertheless, we should now be looking for greater depth in the assessment that takes place. As Tim Oates, Group Director of Assessment Research and Development at Cambridge Assessment, said in 2014:

'Study fewer things in greater depth, so a deeper understanding of central concepts and ideas can be developed. Assessment should focus on that.'

We know that levels are a poor indicator of what a student could or couldn't do. They do not provide sufficient information for other adults or parents to understand accurately what students need support with. Although they were designed specifically to do the reverse, levels are simply labels for students.

Conversely, self- and peer-assessment provide the perfect opportunity to build depth into assessment. Learners need to develop assessment skills and it is worth investing time in this, particularly as part of a whole-school, department or phase approach. So how can we ensure that self- and peer-assessment are valid tools that will decrease workload in this context?

Self–assessment and peer–assessment explained

You should never use self- and peer-assessment simply because your school or an observer insists that you do. It should form a concrete evidence base for students' learning and be a motivational and reflective opportunity for each individual child in your class. Both self- and peer-assessment are skills that need to be taught so that they become a routine in your lessons. They are part of the permanent dialogue between teaching and learning. They also form within the learner an ongoing process of:

Questioning ➡ **Evaluating** ➡ **Reconceptualising**

This is an inquiry cycle that develops the cognitive process.

Of course, self- and peer-assessment can sometimes be unreliable, with the largest deviation found among students who do not understand the success criteria or the objectives. But whose assessment has more value? Is it the teacher's assessment or the learner's assessment? Arguments could be made for both. So, in order to provide a more accurate snapshot of the child's learning, perhaps a balance between the two is required. Of course, the next question is: what is the correct balance?

Before you mark an important piece of work, you should try to get to the point where it has gone through the following cycle of assessment and improvement:

Self ➡ **Peer** ➡ **Self**

Then you should take in the piece of work and assess it from your point of view, as the teacher.

But how do we get our students to self- and peer-assess successfully? Here are some strategies you can use to get started.

Student–friendly mark scheme

Create a student-friendly mark scheme at the beginning of term and ask students to mark their own work and that of their peers against it each time you want them to self- or peer-assess. You could also share with them your simple, five-symbol marking code that you developed in Section 1, Idea 4, p. 23 so they are marking in the same way as you! This may take a bit of time at the start of term but will save you plenty of marking later on.

Highlighting

Give your students a set of coloured pens. Ask them to highlight on their work where they have shown evidence of different skills according to the requirements of the mark scheme you gave them.

Margin marking

To get students used to assessing their own work, put a mark in the margin indicating how many mistakes there are in a particular paragraph or section. Then ask students to look back through their work to find the mistakes and correct them.

EVIDENCE

In their article 'Formative Assessment and Self-regulated Learning: A Model and Seven Principles of Good Feedback Practice', David Nicol and Debra Macfarlane-Dick report on research they conducted in relation to formative assessment and feedback. They suggest that students should be seen 'as having a proactive rather than a reactive role in generating and using feedback' and offer seven recommendations for teachers that will help students take control of their learning:

1. 'Clarify what good performance is

2. Facilitate self-assessment

3. Deliver high quality feedback information

4. Encourage teacher and peer dialogue

5. Encourage positive motivation and self-esteem

6. Provide opportunities to close the gap

7. Use feedback to improve teaching.' (Nicol and Macfarlane-Dick, 2006)

As highlighted in the research, students can only achieve learning objectives if they understand what these goals are in the first place and if they take some ownership of and can assess their own performance. In order to facilitate this, teachers must create structured opportunities for self-assessment. Feedback from the teacher is also essential in helping students to develop self-regulation because teachers are 'more effective in identifying errors or misconceptions in students' work than peers or the students themselves'. However, the report recommends that feedback should be more of a 'dialogue rather than

Mastery marking

We saw in Section 1, Idea 5, p. 29 how a teacher could use mastery marking – the practice of refusing to accept a piece of work until it is of a specific quality. It helps students achieve their full potential and gives them a real opportunity to secure the knowledge required for the assessment. Take this one step further and ask students to 'mastery mark' each other's work. The students give each other verbal feedback until they agree that the piece of work is of the required standard. If this can be sustained, then you will have truly accomplished mastery of your own workload!

Now, if we could get everyone to accept verbal feedback as an immediate and valuable method of marking in the classroom – that does not need to be evidenced with written comments or stamps in books – we'd all be starting a revolution!

information transmission' in order to improve the effectiveness of feedback and ensure students understand and can act on it. Verbal feedback and 'live-marking' would be good examples of this.

The report also draws upon research (including Carol Dweck's 'growth mindset') that suggests that 'high-stakes assessment' can have a negative impact on students' motivation and self-esteem because it focuses students on performance and not learning goals. The report therefore suggests that several 'low-stakes assessment tasks' are more beneficial in helping students to self-regulate.

Crucially, the report provides five key strategies to 'close the gap between current and desired performance', all the while reducing teacher workload. These include:

1. Providing feedback and allowing students to resubmit work.

2. Using 'two stage assignments' where feedback on the first stage informs the second stage.

3. Modelling tasks.

4. Providing 'action points'.

5. Asking students to identify their own action points in groups.

Finally, the report argues that 'teachers themselves need good data about how students are progressing' in order to help their students self-regulate. Other strategies that will help reduce teacher workload are also cited and include students requesting the feedback they would like to receive and asking students to highlight where they are having difficulties.

It's not good enough!

IDEA SNAPSHOT

In previous ideas, we've seen that feedback is one of the most effective ways to improve learning, but we should recognise that not everything can (or should) be marked. To strike a balance between quality and quantity of marking, let's take a look at what work we should not be marking and how verbal feedback can help.

This can be a hard one for us teachers. We are so fixated on marking every piece of work that our students produce because an external audience may at some point question the feedback that they see or do not see. But by the time we've made it through the stack of books, weeks or months after students have submitted them to us for marking, the opportunity to discuss and improve work in class will already have passed us by!

We need to strike a balance between quality and quantity. Teachers need to go back to 'the big picture' as discussed in Section 1, Idea 1, p. 6. Why are you marking? What will add most value to the teaching and learning? Where does the curriculum fit into the assessment? After all, the curriculum should be driving teaching and assessment, not the other way around. You will see evidence of this not being the case in schools where every classroom is testing students at a particular time of year, rather than according to the needs of the curriculum.

I've never been a fan of marking, but what teacher is? I do, however, recognise that marking is my greatest planning tool. The more I have delved into policy and workload strategy, the more I have been thinking seriously and cognitively about my own marking. Dare I say, I am actually enjoying marking now that I understand it better than I first did as a newly qualified teacher and a young middle leader. I now understand the impact that marking can have on student progress, as well as (if streamlined) how marking can appropriately and sensitively reduce workload.

Marking should:

- develop high-quality assessment
- develop diagnostic feedback across all subjects
- be realistic in terms of workload
- be approached with common sense
- work for students and teachers from the outset.

So, with all this in mind, let's look at what we SHOULD NOT be marking to give teachers the freedom to mark less but with greater impact.

What should not be marked?

The first thing to say is that you should never be afraid of telling a student that their work is not good enough for you to spend time marking it. On many occasions, I've refused to collect or mark a piece of work, giving it straight back to a student, if it is not up to the standard I would expect from them. This has not only saved me huge amounts of time, but also forces the student to self-assess their own work, improving it and developing the requisite knowledge for the assessment. It will also encourage them to take more pride in their work next time!

Here are some other suggestions for reducing the quantity of work we mark in favour of the quality of our marking.

- Do not provide extensive or unnecessary written dialogue. In particular, you should avoid 'triple marking', whereby a teacher first marks the work, then a student responds to a teacher and the teacher is expected either to re-mark the work or reply to the student's actions. Research from the EEF says 'there is no strong evidence that "acknowledgement" steps in either dialogic or triple impact marking will promote learning' (Elliott et al., 2016).

- Do not bother leaving comments such as 'well done' or 'good' on students' work. It is a waste of time. Say it in person when returning the work to the student and only write clear action points in their book. Better still, reduce your workload and try the yellow box (see Section 1, Idea 3, p. 17) or simply give instant verbal feedback.

- Do not promise students, parents or colleagues a particular frequency of marking work. It will mean you are marking for the sake of adhering to this schedule. As discussed in Section 1, Idea 4, p. 23, marking should be regular and proportionate to the curriculum. It's that simple.

- Do not mark every single page of work and avoid tick-and-flick. Instead, simply leave the work blank and communicate to the student exactly what will be assessed.

If you are still desperate to mark as much of your students' work as possible, we can increase the amount we mark, while still reducing the amount of time we spend on marking, by swapping extensive written feedback for verbal feedback.

Verbal feedback

Primary Deputy Headteacher Jeremy Hannay has said 'the idea that written feedback is the best and only kind needs to be put to rest. Not only will this help children learn, it'll reduce teacher workload'. It is a wonderful quote first shared with me last year. It has resonated with me ever since.

Hannay shows how poorly interpreted research and old Grim Reaper policy have driven schools 'to adopt widely unsubstantiated (and sometimes outright wrong) ideas:

1. That written feedback is the most valuable type.

2. That the best written feedback is a conversation between pupil and teacher.

3. That feedback must be evidenced in a book to "count'" towards progress, evidence, etc. (Hannay, 2016)

For me, the sooner that schools move towards verbal feedback (with demonstrable quality and aplomb), the better for teacher workload and every child. Imagine this: instant verbal feedback, provided there and then, with a meaningful and motivating return to the student, but without a single pen stroke! And how would we know it was working? Well, we all know what a good teacher looks like, right? And it's not just at the end of term when the examination results are published…

Verbal feedback stamps

Stamps on students' work that indicate that you have given verbal feedback are a by-product of a broken system that requires teachers to evidence feedback to internal and external observers. They are absolute nonsense! If you have been told to evidence a particular school approach within a lesson or every twenty minutes to show your leadership team that students are doing X, Y or Z, your creativity as a teacher is being stifled.

Of course, every school needs consistency and with some flexibility, a whole-school approach can in fact provide teachers with more autonomy. I've seen both sides of this coin, and it is not something that can be driven by school leaders alone. Every teacher, yes, *every teacher* in every classroom must meet common expectations if you and your school are to thrive.

'Hang on!' you ask, 'Didn't you just say we need teachers to be more autonomous and schools to be less top-down in their approaches?'

Well, yes, I did, but at a cost. No matter what you are trying to achieve, if there is no consistency and common sense applied across the school – by every individual teacher – any sensible approach to working smarter, not harder, will be lost. Therefore, if your school insists (though hopefully they wouldn't) that every teacher uses a verbal feedback stamp, then I'd recommend doing it for the sake of long-term autonomy, whilst challenging any unforeseen nonsense with evidence and research. In fact, why not conduct your own action research and leave the report on your headteacher's desk?

Advantages and disadvantages

The advantages (yes, there are some) and disadvantages of using verbal feedback stamps:

Advantages	Disadvantages
It's quick!	It's a total waste of time!
It's a visual reminder for you and the student.	It adds no value to the learning.
It's proof to school leaders and inspectors that you are (actually) speaking to your students.	It's proof that you are stamping for evidence trails and not for you or your student.
Erm...?	It adds to the marking frenzy, your workload and, worst of all, supports watchdog fads to 'show progress'.

With the rise of mobile technology, I have experimented with mobile apps in class to record verbal feedback and capture conversations I have with my students about their work. This gives me, the students and any observers (if *really* necessary) a lasting record of the feedback but it is still quick to do and engaging for students.

Remember, you do not need to mark every single piece of work that your students produce and you certainly do not need to return everything to students with extensive written feedback. Not only will this save you time, but it will improve the quality of your marking and ensure it has a greater impact on your students' learning.

In May 2017, the EEF published a research summary on 'Feedback' as part of its Teaching and Learning Toolkit (EEF, 2017c). In consideration of the evidence, the report concluded:

- Effective feedback 'should be specific, accurate and clear (e.g. "It was good because you…", rather than just "correct")'.

- Feedback should be about 'challenging tasks' because this will 'emphasise the importance of effort and perseverance as well as be more valued by the pupils'.

- Teachers should consider 'the challenge of implementing feedback effectively and consistently'.

This supports the idea that not every single piece of work a student produces needs to be marked. As teachers, we should be more selective about the tasks we choose to give feedback on because marking some tasks will have more impact than marking others. This will reduce the amount of marking that we do, giving us more time to ensure that our marking is genuinely useful when we do decide to feed back on a task. There is no point simply giving a cursory tick or cross or scribbling a hurried 'good' on every piece of work. We must sacrifice quantity for quality, allowing ourselves the opportunity to provide in-depth feedback that will help our students to progress.

The EEF report also discusses a number of studies that are currently investigating 'the importance of quick verbal feedback' that aim to 'inform decisions about marking'. The results cannot come quickly enough!

There is currently very little evidence and research into verbal feedback. If we revisit the report the EEF published with the University of Oxford in April 2016, which reviews the literature in the area of marking and feedback, it appears that there are no studies that 'have compared the impact of written dialogue to verbal dialogue for this purpose'.

There is no doubt that schools require more evidence in this field. I've thought about conducting some of my own research just to help alleviate the workload crisis and also dispel Grim Reaper rumours that written feedback trumps everything else a teacher does. Why should we accept that a teacher must mark students' books after every other lesson and return feedback after the event itself has been lost? I accept that this will not be the case for every subject, lesson or topic, but we must move with the times. Verbal feedback – albeit with a common vernacular and a script to aid improvement – is required to support progress in a classroom. All teachers and students will be worse off until we have wider evidence to support its validity in our classrooms.

Section 1: Summary

What we have been looking for in this section of the book are smarter ideas to reduce workload and improve the impact of our marking. No one can argue with that, surely? We know that marking will never disappear from the life of a teacher but we also know that the landscape of teaching is in flux and how we go about assessing students and equipping them in the classroom is evolving. Remember, too, that there are psychological factors, such as motivation, understanding needs and reflecting on the cognitive and emotional aspects of learning that underpin your practice.

Unfortunately, the research we need is not yet in the eyes and ears of every school inspector or school leader, so if you are lucky enough to be part of action research in your school or you discover a hidden gem to help combat teacher workload and change the marking dialogue, share it widely and loudly.

To conclude this chapter, here is a summary of the ten high-impact, evidence-based ideas I have suggested to improve your marking:

1. Develop a 'secure overview' before setting and marking an assessment. Consider where you are in the curriculum, the starting point, the progress and the context of each student and the purpose of setting and marking this specific piece of work. The curriculum should determine your assessment strategy, not the other way around, and this will help ensure your marking impacts on teaching and learning.

2. Use the powerful words 'not yet' in your marking to motivate students to improve their learning and develop a growth mindset.

3. Create a culture of live-marking in your classroom to help your students progress more quickly and to reduce your workload outside of lesson time.

4. Ensure you are using a marking code that works for both you and your students and remains in line with school policy to help your students progress and save you time.

5. Encourage a culture of redrafting in your classroom where not every piece of work is the finished article and mistakes are used to improve learning.

6. Use marking and assessment to spot the 'gap' in your students' learning, then go back and re-teach anything that students haven't quite grasped.

7. Ask students to identify gaps in their own learning and understand how they can 'find and fix' mistakes and problem areas themselves.

8. Moderate student work and marking as an individual teacher, a department or an entire school to inform curriculum planning and monitor progress, but never do so without taking context into account.

9. Make your marking smarter and ensure your students are working harder than you are by introducing them to self-assessment and peer-assessment. Take time at the beginning of term to teach them how to do this effectively and you will save yourself time for the rest of the year.

10. Don't give extensive written feedback on every single piece of student work. Be selective about the tasks you choose to mark and use verbal feedback to provide your students with quality, not quantity, in your marking.

Section 2: PLAN.

When I was a young and inexperienced teacher, I spent hours and hours planning lessons. It's a shame to see this still being expected of teachers twenty years later, especially among those with experience. Schools I have worked in would insist that teachers write lessons out in detail and then submit the plans to observers one week in advance. And as a newly qualified teacher, this was expected for every lesson. I've also heard of primary school teachers having to complete weekly overviews and being asked to submit these ahead of each week of teaching.

Can you believe some schools still ask their teachers to do this? It's like asking all drivers to resit their theory test every time they jump into a car to drive it away. It's worthy knowledge but we know drivers generally get better with road practice, and theory is useless without the practice. And why do we still insist in all routes into teaching that trainee teachers provide detailed lesson scripts that lead observers through lesson sequences, when the observers are not the ones actually teaching the lesson?

Is there a need for lesson planning on mass-produced templates? Is there a need for any teacher to write – never mind submit – a lesson plan, other than when going through initial teacher induction? It's a crazy mindset we have in our profession. I'm all for developing and tweaking practice, but where is the freedom to trust teachers and help reduce their workload as they develop a repertoire and gain experience? After many years in the classroom, teachers should be permitted to rely on this experience to save them time when it comes to preparing for lessons. In her blog, Jude Enright writes about how little time she had to plan lessons as a member of the senior leadership team in her school, meaning she relied on 'door knob lessons' – lessons she planned while turning the door knob to enter the classroom:

> 'When I joined [senior leadership], my lessons were invariably door knob lessons. You have so much extra to worry about, to solve, that you have very little time to spare and plan lessons.' (Enright, 2013)

In this section of the book, I provide you with a range of options to consider for lesson planning. We will question what we've always done, as well as consider cognitive processes to help better understand the mechanics needed behind planning to inform not only what a teacher needs to teach, but how and why.

For the past ten years, I've been using the **5 Minute Lesson Plan** to frame the process of planning on one page. It's perfect for working smarter and definitely reduces workload. All you need to do is trial it – nothing works for everyone, remember – and if you like it, suggest using it in your school as a framework for all lesson planning to help remove any unnecessary bureaucracy and burden placed upon you and your colleagues. It's a great model and it has evolved deeply in recent years, not because of changes to 'external accountability' or other phrases often bandied about in the education sector, but because I've rediscovered the importance of planning lessons the right way.

Find my 5 Minute Lesson Plan here:
www.5minutelessonplan.co.uk

The right way

Three weeks into my job as a deputy headteacher, I sat down with a school inspector and opened a file given to me by my predecessor. To my horror, there were lesson plans spanning three pages in length. I was mortified! There was clearly much work to be done to change habits of thought and eliminate unnecessary tasks.

The main issue with lesson plans is that what is written in the plan is not what happens in the classroom. We know that students can be very unpredictable, which is why it's important that teachers learn from experience and are always adapting to meet the needs of their students in every lesson. It is vital for teachers to plan, but it's impossible to be able to predict every detail of a lesson. What teachers can do instead is roadmap the lesson as a whole and target what students can learn on this intended journey.

I recall when a middle leader came into my classroom to observe me. In fact, it was only last year. 'Do you have a lesson plan?' he asked. I smiled, said 'no' and carried on teaching the class. I was modelling to colleagues what I also wanted from them – to plan their lessons for the students in front of them, not for a passing observer.

So, despite my obvious desire to quash actual lesson plans, this does not mean we should all ignore the process of planning or encourage new teachers to ignore it. The need for planning will never go away; it is a vital part of learning to teach and gauging what works. We should encourage our teachers to have 'planning schemes', drawing out learning pathways from greater curriculum plans that map out key aspects of the knowledge and skills to be taught. This grand scheme can then be used to filter what needs to be learnt in class. 'Stickability' – or 'what learning should stick' – is what lesson planning should hinge upon and is something I explain in much more detail in Section 2, Idea 4, p. 78. This all feeds into a lesson plan of sorts, but not a one-off lesson plan written out in detail on paper.

The thinking process taking place in your mind when you plan lessons provides a lot of detail that doesn't necessarily need recording. Instead, you should try to capture the key elements of learning in a simple planning framework, such as the 5 Minute Lesson Plan. What I believe is great about focused and simple lesson planning is that it helps us concentrate on what's important. We are not necessarily focused on *what* we are teaching, but *why* we are teaching it (see Section 2, Idea 2, p. 67). More explicitly, we are thinking about the learning itself, rather than classroom activities.

The planning process

Planning is a process, not a product. It has one purpose: to enable high-quality delivery, which meets the needs of all students. So, before you start reading my ideas on the process of lesson planning, take a moment to reflect on what you think teachers should be planning for in the various stages of a lesson. Use the table on the next page to record your thoughts.

TABLE OVERLEAF

The planning process	What you will be doing and what the students will be doing
Start of lesson	
After initial start	
While students are working	
Towards the end of the lesson	
End of lesson	

Did filling out this table help you to frame the process of lesson planning or did it at least make you start questioning your planning habits? Once you've read the ten ideas I present on lesson planning in this section, revisit your completed table and see whether you'd do anything differently in light of my suggestions. Let me know using the hashtag #MarkPlanTeach.

Now, let's get started!

A cognitive process

IDEA SNAPSHOT

Planning a lesson is a cognitive process – a reflective process – and is not a form filling exercise. It is important that teachers always think about the bigger picture. How does your lesson plan fit into your scheme of work or the topic that you are teaching? What knowledge are students coming to the lesson with and what would you like them to take away? In this idea, I encourage readers to reflect on what students should *learn*, not what they should *do*, as the starting point in the process of lesson planning.

L esson planning is a learning curve and teachers will often adapt methods handed down to them by their mentors or enforced by school policies. There is no single solution for planning, no silver bullet or exemplar methodology, other than a teacher trying out different techniques and learning from their successes and failures. This pattern of trial and error will be repeated with each new intake of students and every time a teacher moves to a new school. Crucially, when evaluating a lesson and considering ways to move forward, teachers must remain reflective. This is an essential characteristic in our profession.

It is vital that teachers understand planning as a course of action, a process of unfolding teaching and learning into something that is accessible for those sitting in the classroom. It is a thinking process, and developing good habits of thought about lesson planning is of fundamental importance for all teachers. How to master lesson planning is a long journey.

When you start planning a lesson, you should first think about the bigger picture. It's important to consider what's going on in the classroom before the actual lesson, and where you see yourself currently with the students. Breaking down what you want students to learn can often reveal skills or knowledge they have to acquire and that need to be taught.

As obvious as it sounds, your planning must first consider *what students should learn* before giving any consideration to what you want the students to *do* to reach this goal. Throughout each stage of lesson planning, ask yourself 'why?' and connect the learning episodes with the intended outcomes in mind (see Section 2, Idea 2, p. 67 for more on this).

What you should not do

All too frequently, planning starts from the wrong place. Teachers find an excellent activity or resource and do their utmost to integrate it into their lesson plan, re-engineering the schemes of work in order to make their lesson workable. It's backward planning and takes away the hard work already done in curriculum planning. There's nothing wrong with integrating enticing resources and activities into lessons — it's what makes teachers creative and enjoy their work — but it should never be in place of planning lessons properly.

In *Lean Lesson Planning*, Peps Mccrea suggests that the planning process should have a 'lean mindset', meaning it should be all about quality and not about quantity. All too often, teachers start planning lessons by thinking about *how* students will learn something, without first considering where students are and what goal they need to reach next. The bigger picture is often not examined. Mccrea, an experienced lecturer in teacher education – someone who has the responsibility to impart lifelong habits for great lesson planning – says that there are two 'classic traps' that teachers can fall into:

1. 'Activity-focused planning'
2. 'Coverage-focused planning' (Mccrea, 2015).

Headteacher Alex Atherton adds a third: 'over-planning'. It's hard to argue against these, so let's look at each in turn.

'Activity–focused planning': when did you last do this?

You come across (or try to find) a good activity and then reverse engineer the lesson objectives to match the likely outcomes of the activity. Over time, this can become an exercise in keeping students busy and leads to more *doing* than *learning*.

'Coverage–focused planning': how much do we rely on others?

This begins with using another teacher's learning objectives (from a colleague or a textbook, for example), rather than considering your own students' needs and how the objectives could be interpreted or adapted for them. Over time, this can become an exercise in getting through the curriculum or covering everything required for an assessment, rather than understanding your own lesson planning and the students in front of you. There is a need for off-the-shelf lesson planning to help improve teacher workload, but this shouldn't be used as an excuse for teachers who can't be bothered to read the curriculum plans or who rely on ready-made PowerPoint presentations.

'Over–planning': how often have you done this?

Too many activities? Too many objectives? I have definitely been guilty of this before and I'm sure every teacher has too at some point in their career. You fail to break down lesson objectives (and no, they don't need to be written down on the whiteboard or in students' books, or worse, checked off at the end of the lesson to see if students almost hit the lesson plan targets) and then realise during the lesson that you are trying to cover too much, or that you have not differentiated. Over-planning generally leads to under-learning; the pressure to match what you had intended to teach with

How do you like to plan your lessons?

How important is it to you to have every learning episode planned out? Do you stick to your plans most of the time, or are they simply a tool to help you crystallise your ideas? How do you store, organise or reuse your plans? Do they end up in a folder tucked into a drawer or hidden away somewhere on your computer to then be forgotten about or regurgitated next year when teaching the same project with another class?

Generally, I think lesson plans should stay in the mind but they can of course be beautifully crafted or just roughly sketched out. Action research I have carried out with Angel Solutions took a sample of nearly 500 anonymised lesson plans created on www.5minutelessonplan.co.uk by teachers from all over the world. We analysed how many learning episodes teachers chose to include in each of their plans and whether these were primarily student or teacher led.

Overall, the number of learning episodes in each plan varied. However, it's striking that nearly half of the plans in the sample (44% to be precise) included a total of four learning episodes. There were also more student-led episodes than teacher-led episodes. Lessons with four learning episodes were more likely to be led by a teacher in the first episode and by students in the last episode.

What is striking about the evidence is that more often than not, the teacher facilitated the beginning of the lesson, and this introduction was often then followed by a period of students leading their own learning. Fascinating! But I wonder how this differs in subjects and in school settings? I'm sure lesson planning varies dramatically for teachers who teach A-level students and teachers working with Reception classes. So for me, what's important is the process of planning, regardless of how many learning episodes you plan, whether you keep your lesson plans in your mind or put them down on paper, and what you do with them after the lesson has been taught.

the actual outcomes of thirty individuals every lesson already only has a one in thirty chance of being successful. That's very slim odds.

What you should do

To avoid these traps, ask yourself not 'how can we get to X, Y or Z?' but 'where are the students starting from?'. Once this is established, planning can help shape where you want students to get to in the lesson, and subject knowledge, resources and activities can be introduced around the purpose of the lesson. 'Wait', I hear you ask, 'how will I know when students are there?' and 'why is it vital that they reach X, Y or Z?'. Once a simple framework is established in the mind of a teacher, the final eureka moment is knowing how to engineer a method for students to reach the goal of a lesson.

If this all needs to be written down in a lesson plan, it can hopefully be for your benefit only and not for any observer. Even better, if the script needs to be recorded for the lesson itself, it should take less than five minutes to do because in your mind, the hard work has already been completed. This also helps you to communicate your lesson plan to your students effectively.

If you cannot describe your lesson plan in less than thirty seconds, it's already overcomplicated. You should aim for excessive clarity and precision in your mind, so you can articulate what you want your students to learn and what you want them to do so that they learn it. Explanations should be phrased in such a way that students will quickly understand what they are aiming for. This is the bigger picture; hard graft, namely the process of planning, filtered into a succinct thirty-second lesson plan. As Jim Smith says in his book *The Lazy Teacher's Handbook*, as you reduce the amount of time you spend actually teaching, you can start to observe the learning more (Smith, 2010).

Lesson planning: an art or a science?

I've always believed that teaching is an art form but that over the years, I have adapted my techniques considerably and have made my teaching style a science. But my views could be challenged easily. As Alexander Makedon argues in his paper 'Is Teaching a Science or an Art?', 'whether teaching is an art or a science depends on which definition of teaching we adopt, or what we think the goals of teaching should be'. He does, however, suggest that this is a question worth pondering:

> 'If art is not different from science, then it makes no sense that we should have two different terms in our language to describe essentially the same thing [...] There must be certain underlying principles or practices in science which we can't reject without at the same time becoming unscientific, and the same may be said regarding art.' (Makedon, 1990)

So, is lesson planning an art form or a science? Perhaps it's both? Or neither?! For Mccrea, planning is a form of 'architecture', an 'exercise in design [that is] a stormy marriage of process and creativity. Where science and art collide.' Mccrea writes *Lean Lesson Planning* as a deliberate attempt to make the lesson planning process simple with a roadmap of three acts:

Act I: 'Lean foundations' introduces the 'meanings, mindsets and habits underpinning the lean approach'.

Act II: 'Habits for planning' details the 'core habits of lean planning'.

Act III: 'Habits for growing' provides strategies for growing excellent classroom practice.

Act II begins with a chapter on 'backwards design', which is poignant for us in terms of the cognitive process of lesson planning. Mccrea argues that 'backwards design' leads to better solutions. This is something I have grappled with in my senior leadership roles in school. Often, school leaders need to be well ahead of the workforce in terms of whole-school deadlines, providing resources and guidance to their staff in time for various new initiatives or professional development to take place. We have to plan events or activities with the end goal in mind. This is very similar to what we do as teachers in the classroom, and although the time I spend teaching has decreased as my responsibilities have increased, the habits I acquired in the formative years of my career are still very much evident in how I manage senior leadership processes.

In fact, I discovered a strategy that enhanced my planning while undertaking my master's degree over ten years ago. It is something I apply in all aspects of school life. 'What?', 'Why?', 'How?', 'What if?' and 'When?' are the simplest, yet most effective, questions to ask yourself when forward or backward planning. This simple questioning technique can be implemented when planning lessons or teacher training days, when producing policies or when leading school meetings.

Planning with the end goal in mind enables planning for optimum learning. It's a matter of changing the lens and sharply focusing everything you do on *learning*, rather than on activities you want your students to do. Instead of 'what do I need the students to do?' or 'why do I need the students to do this?', ask yourself, 'why do I need students to *learn* this?'. This self-regulatory reflective thought really does sharpen the teacher. Once you've made this leap, you can then start to hone in on the cognitive processes of lesson planning.

Following on from this idea on cognition, I will unpick the stages required for lesson planning and suggest a process that all teachers should consider.

Psychology and... reflection

If 'I teach and you learn' was as simple as it sounds, then absolutely anyone without any qualifications could be a teacher. But it's not that simple. Teaching and learning are complex. One of the challenges of being a teacher is responding to individual differences and dispositions within groups. To do this, you need a plan. To create a plan, you need to reflect – you need to be a 'reflective practitioner'. The process of reflection is of critical importance in any needs-related context.

Teachers are called upon to be reflective practitioners – raising consciousness of the meaning of their own experience. Reflection is a higher order psychological activity that involves the perceiver interacting with the perceived: it is a form of subjective critique where we step back from our familiar world in order to establish new meanings and construct new responses. When reflecting, teachers are encouraged to problematise experience – to become deliberately puzzled – so that they can build new repertoires for teaching. A teacher can engage in 'reflection-in-action' or 'reflection-on-action'. The former is an analytical response that occurs in situ and the latter occurs retrospectively post activity; both are context dependent and context respondent.

CONTINUES OVER PAGE

Schön (1983) is a key initiator of the discourse of teacher as reflective practitioner but his model is open to critique. Firstly, he posits reflection as an individual activity but teachers do not exist as individual entities; they exist in communities of practice. Therefore, group reflection that is participatory is required alongside individual reflection. Also, a reflective practitioner may well think about the 'doing' of practice but this does not necessarily mean they are a reflective theoriser. It can also be proposed that teaching is so complex that it calls for constructions and responses that are not based upon the intellectual processes of critical reflection at all. The proposition here is that teaching involves an anatomy of intuition and reflection, as a process can stifle intuition and block creativity.

The process of reflection, with its emphasis upon the critical analysis of predicaments, challenges and dilemmas, ensures that both experience and pedagogy remain under constant scrutiny. As teachers become more reflective, they also become more reflexive: continually engaged in researching their own practice and interrogating their own theoretical frameworks. By definition, the job of a reflective practitioner is never finished.

– Dr Tim O'Brien

The 'why?' test

IDEA SNAPSHOT

Once you have identified what you want students to learn in your lesson (Section 2, Idea 1, p. 61), you should then turn your attention to how your students will get there. You should apply the 'why?' test to all the learning activities you plan to include to ensure each one will deliver the learning you want your students to achieve, in the time you have allocated to it. As teachers, we must establish a mechanism for our students to understand *why* they are learning things, rather than just *what* they are learning. This will not only help to deepen their understanding but will also increase engagement in the classroom.

As adults, we can all recognise the time in a child's life when they repeatedly respond, 'Why?' to everything that you say. As a parent, this can be very frustrating – particularly on a car journey – but it is, thankfully, a phase that normally only lasts for a brief period of time. Nevertheless, after years of frustration and trying to quash this exasperating habit, it is strange for me to admit that asking 'why?' is something I would promote for all teachers – and for every child!

'Why?' is a more sophisticated question than 'what?'. It seeks a greater understanding of the world around us. It helps us to unpick concepts and problems using a higher order of thinking and deepens our learning. Although we don't know the exact science behind how we learn best, we do know that understanding – or at least asking ourselves – 'why?' requires a greater depth of thought than simply being asked to recall via 'what?'.

Let's look at how this applies to lesson planning.

The dangers of over-planning

As we saw in Section 2, Idea 1, p. 61, over-planning can be a very common problem among teachers, especially when they are going to be observed. This tends to lead them to focus on activities in order to satisfy observers and their checklists, rather than on episodes that are intended to have a genuine impact on students' learning. But how can you recognise that you are falling into this trap? Well, the first quality control check is simple: ask yourself whether you believe that you are spending too much time lesson planning.

If the answer is 'yes', what external factors are influencing this? If it's likely to be line manager or school expectations, then workload and teacher mental health must be questioned. If this isn't the problem, then you should make sure your lesson activities are focused on learning and not on control. Over-planning and teaching to the middle (rather than differentiating successfully) can be signs that student behaviour is hindering teaching and therefore impacting on the quality of the learning that can take place. Worse, when teachers are dealing with a difficult class, control can feel like the best (or only) way to share knowledge.

In this case, simplifying planning is easier said than done. Particularly in the first few weeks of teaching a new class, simplification is something that is etched into the dreams of all newly qualified teachers. They often question how more experienced teachers can waltz into lessons with no more than a board pen and have children lapping up their every word and powering through reams and reams of work.

All teachers need some time to gel with their students. Lesson plans often go out the window in the first few classes, even for the most experienced teachers. But regardless of the circumstances, a focus on learning should always be your long-term aim. Rather than teaching to control, in order to then be able to teach, let's think about how planning can lead to a heightened sense of confidence in being prepared for a lesson and in keeping students readily engaged. When I say engaged, I don't mean making a lesson loads of fun and including various wacky tasks involving you and your students singing and dancing on the tables. Getting students engaged in their own learning is hard earned and can only be secured with routine, rigour and recognition of hard work. This is where the 'why?' test comes into play.

Using the 'why?' test in lesson planning

When planning a lesson, ask yourself 'so why are we doing this?' about every single activity you include and question the length of time you allocate to it. This will help you check that the activities are supporting you to deliver the learning you want to achieve and whether there is a more efficient way of doing it. If an activity is not making a significant difference to the teaching and learning in the time you've allotted to it, then drop it. If this becomes habit, you'll start to master the art of planning for learning. Once this technique is embedded, you'll find yourself enjoying a sense of freedom in your day-to-day time management, as lesson planning will feel much more worthwhile and less onerous.

You should also make sure you can explain the 'why?' behind each element of a lesson, clearly and succinctly to your students. This will improve their understanding of their own learning and help keep them engaged for longer, as they will appreciate the importance of each task. You can support the 'why?' of a task through modelling and exemplar work and if you can bring these two things together, you will start to cultivate the roots of a very special classroom. Let me explain how this can be done.

Learning objectives

How often do you question your learning objectives? The precision of your language really counts in making learning stick but this does not mean that students should copy down objectives or that you even need to have any objectives at all. I know, radical, right?

A practice commonly subscribed to by teachers is to 'publish' learning objectives at the start of a lesson and collectively share them so that everyone knows what the purpose of the lesson is. Students then routinely copy them out into their books and there's your evidence. Objectives covered.

However, as Dr Debra Kidd points out in her brilliant book, *Teaching: Notes from the Front Line*, this isn't always the best use of lesson time:

> 'Across schools all over the country, little clones write objectives in their books copied from boards plastered with two letters, LO, or two words, WALT (We Are Learning Today) and WILF (What I'm Looking For) […] Even if in every lesson, just two minutes are spent on this, that is 10 minutes per day, 50 minutes per week and 32.5 hours of learning lost per year!' (Kidd, 2014)

But don't despair! This certainly isn't the only way of doing things. In *The Spider Strategy: Six Steps to Outstanding*, Marcella McCarthy devotes a whole chapter to 'purpose' and shares one strategy that specifically involves *not* sharing learning objectives. She calls this the 'Invisible Sun' (McCarthy, 2014).

The idea behind this strategy is to write down or record your learning objectives (rather than just keeping them in your head), but have them hidden from view until the end of the lesson. It's something worth testing out in your own classroom. It allows teachers to dive straight in and teach, and it gives students the task of trying to unpick what the learning objectives are as they move through the lesson. A similar strategy would be to provide students with an answer and ask them to work out the original question.

Would you feel comfortable doing this?

It's certainly not for the faint-hearted or struggling teacher. So why do it all? The purpose is that students have to think harder about what they are doing and why they are doing it. Effective teaching and secure behaviour management can embed a culture for learning where students really have to work hard to understand not only what, but why and how they are going to learn.

It turns the lesson into a mystery that the students have to solve and that keeps them engaged right to the end. It's not for everyone, but it is an approach worth considering. And it certainly beats students copying out lesson objectives at the start of every class.

Modelling

Finding ways to get students to meet and master lesson objectives is tough. Goal setting or sharing lesson objectives can have a meaningful impact on student progress, but not if how you share or record objectives is prescribed in a specific way that adheres to checklists or that is used to beat teachers over the head. It would be my advice that every teacher chooses what suits their students and subject, and selects when (and when not) to share, copy or record lesson goals. Regardless, in all examples, whether for a one-off lesson or for a series of lessons for a project, teachers must *model* the success criteria, namely why we are learning what we are learning, in some shape or form.

This has been a feature of some of the best teaching that I have observed. No matter how high the expectation, how brilliantly the students were working on their own or in groups, or how good the students' work was, there was always an explicit model of the success criteria for the lesson or project. Whenever I spoke to students in these classes, they were *always* clear about what they were trying to achieve and exactly what that could look like.

Why this is so important is clear. How often do you hear students say, 'Do we have to, Sir?' or 'Why are we doing this, Miss? Can we do this instead?' In terms of planning, teachers teaching to set curriculums must have answers for 'why' students need to learn, for example, trigonometry or the American Civil War of 1861, so that they understand the cognitive need for learning, develop a deeper understanding of these topics and can see how they can apply this knowledge in the future, rather than just being able to regurgitate facts. This relates to cognitive load theory, which links the amount of effort being used in the working memory to how well we learn and retain information in our long-term memory. Understanding 'why' requires students to put in some hard work. It also requires teachers to ensure they offer explanation and detail.

If any teacher can master this, then it's a classroom environment I would love to observe. It is largely an unknown area for teachers and an approach, in terms of a new era of evidence-rich teaching and neuroscience to understand what works and why, in which we are only just scratching the surface.

Tips for modelling success criteria

Here are a few strategies for teachers to model success criteria (the lesson objectives or the 'why?' of learning) and tackle this aspect of teaching:

1. Show what a good piece of work looks like. Talk classwork through and share your thoughts.

2. Celebrate mistakes. Show students what to do when you don't know what to do.

3. Build a classroom climate based on trust and a belief that with good practice, you can get better.

4. Never make assumptions about what the students already know and understand.

5. Model the learning in many ways. Some students will be ready to run; others may need a little guided work.

It isn't one size fits all. It's about providing the right level of scaffold, support and inspiration for your students. That's the true craft of teaching, and it all begins with planning.

Reflection

Now you've read this idea, take a moment to think about some future learning objectives for a class you're teaching at the moment, knowing that the next objective in that class is to build upon what has gone on before. Think about how each objective relates to the aims of the lesson, so you and your students understand *why* this learning is important. Take some inspiration from this idea and scribble down three learning objectives (the big picture) and how they relate to the aim of the lesson in the table on the next page. Share it with me using the hashtag #MarkPlanTeach.

Aim of the lesson:

Learning objective	How it relates to the aim of the lesson
1.	
2.	
3.	

EVIDENCE

Do we really want our students copying learning objectives off the whiteboard and into their books? Every lesson, every day? Is copying out 'L.O. I can… so that…' the only means of sharing with children what they are learning and why they are learning it? These are things that teachers have become accustomed to in recent years, but surely the answer to all these questions is no.

Do school leadership teams want their teachers to write lesson objectives on the board and have them on display every lesson? I don't. However, if I were to seek consistency because it may be viewed favourably by external agencies, then how would I answer that question? Well, my moral answer would still be no. We must ask ourselves whether this habit is present in our schools because we fear what external watchdogs want. Does having a student regurgitate what they are learning in a lesson to a visitor prove that learning is taking place? Of course not. Instead, we should be doing what's right for our students.

As we saw in Section 1, Idea 1, p. 6, John Hattie's research suggests that 'goal setting' has a d = 0.60 impact on student outcomes. This equates to progress of approximately half a grade over an academic year, so learning objectives clearly do have some impact. However, this doesn't mean simply asking students to record objectives or recite them every lesson. Doing so does not demonstrate progress or learning and simply supports evidence chasers, who want to appease observers when they examine students' books. It is not something that should be asked of students anywhere. Instead, we should be making sure students understand *why* they are learning what they are learning to help build a deeper understanding, encourage the application of knowledge and improve engagement. So do share and demonstrate learning objectives, but for goodness sake, don't write them down for anyone other than you or your students.

CONTINUES OVER PAGE

A little research into the matter...

The following extract is by Rachel Preece-Dawson, Senior Leader in a small, rural primary school, who shared her master's thesis with me. Her action research questioned the purpose of sharing lesson objectives with students:

'The overwhelming message from both findings and literature seems to be that pupils and headteachers have very different perceptions of L.O.s and very different understanding of their function. What seems to be of importance to the setting is of little relevance according to the pupils. Further, the headteachers within the LA [local authority] perceive L.O.s as beneficial in focusing pupils, whilst pupils comment that L.O.s can actually put them off learning and make them "switch off" from lessons.

The findings and the literature both show that there is a general notion that schools perceive external accountability to be a driving factor in shaping practice, and yet the frameworks which oversee school inspections are ambiguous in describing expectations. It is interesting, therefore, that the least amount of prescription within the LA is seen in those schools deemed "outstanding" in inspection terms.

It is also of significance that the literature paints a picture of many schools engaging in "surface level" formative assessment: the findings also suggest that there is a lack of deeper understanding of the principles and what is needed to embed formative assessment effectively. Indeed, the findings show that when children engage with the strategies on a deeper level, they are able to reflect more accurately, and with more ownership and engagement, on their own learning.

Further, although pupil perception of differentiation was not a focus of the research, the findings show that pupils have very strong feelings about explicit differentiation: possibly providing a focus for future research.' (Preece-Dawson, 2011)

When it comes to learning objectives, it is clear that one size does not fit all. Teachers should be free to use and share learning objectives in a way that works for them and their students, rather than being forced to comply with requirements dictated by school leadership to meet ambiguous external frameworks. We should use and share learning objectives to enable students to reflect on their learning, take ownership of it and increase their engagement with it.

Storyteller...

IDEA SNAPSHOT

Lessons that are well pitched use imaginative teaching strategies. A colleague (she is now my wife) once told me, 'tell the students a story'. I knew this and had already been doing it subconsciously, but until I'd heard it spoken out loud, I'd never really tried to make it part of my lesson planning. I use this strategy in school assemblies and teacher training events. But how can we integrate engaging strategies into our lesson plans to hold our students' attention while also supporting their learning? Having a clear rationale to work with is essential, and it can make all the difference with lesson planning and delivery in the classroom.

Misbehaviour has no place in the classroom, yet it would be naïve to think it doesn't crop up for every teacher at some point or another, even for the most experienced and even in the least challenging schools. Misbehaviour rears its head in many forms, including non-verbal and non-physical manifestations, which sometimes start outside the classroom (or online) and then arrive in your lesson for you to deal with.

Every teacher must consider how they can secure students' attention in class and ensure all are safe, focused and ready to learn. It can be a challenge for teachers to impart any topic – from the simplest to the most difficult – to thirty students at a time. Whether in a one-off lesson or in a series of lessons as part of a longer-term project, every teacher needs to be able to hold the attention of all their students at any given moment.

It's important for teachers to use engaging teaching techniques at the right time so they can capture the minds of students. Think of a teacher as a television presenter, an actor or a comedy compère standing at the front of a large audience in the West End. How do they hold the attention of the crowd? What are these unwritten rules that just say, 'they've got it'?

For me, teachers who can hold an audience are all of the above. They are comic geniuses, actors and actresses, presenters and politicians all at the same time. They are storytellers who capture the attention and imagination of every student, even the hardest to reach…

Nevertheless, 'engagement' takes a great deal of unnecessary criticism in schools because it's a misnomer for 'having fun' in class. Politicians seek to impart their experiences of school onto classroom policy and processes, assuming what happened thirty years ago will suit the students of today. Teaching is not a mass-production conveyor belt with templated teachers ready to be deployed into any school following a bite-sized teacher training course. Teachers need time to grow and refine their practice, and what external agencies fail to recognise is that every teaching technique, style or resource should be used appropriately, with context and at the right time to ensure maximum impact for students.

For example, there is no point using a tablet just for the sake of completing 'online research' for a project. Nor is there any point in a teacher standing on a row of desks like Robin Williams (a.k.a. English teacher John Keating) in *Dead Poets Society* to 'seize the day', if there is absolutely no chance they could develop students' knowledge and understanding of *A Midsummer Night's Dream* by doing so. They may be able to 'engage' students in the lesson, but are they learning?

However, this is certainly not to say that technology or imaginative teaching strategies should never be used. There is a time and a place for all classroom strategies but we should make sure they will actually help the student make progress before we decide to use them.

Teaching with a story

Have you ever considered teaching with a story? If you haven't already, watch *Dead Poets Society* and think about what Robin Williams does as John Keating to engage his students. He encourages them to 'make [their] lives extraordinary'. It's certainly not a one-off, whimsical idea. Keating's ability throughout the film to engage with his students is hard earned and gradually leads to a place where he is deeply touched by their infamous parting gesture, 'Oh Captain! My Captain', which is the moment he realises his teaching has made a lasting impact.

Stories will help you gain your students' attention at the start of a term and throughout all the lessons you will be together. They build relationships that are exciting and meaningful (without you working too hard) and you can use them to lure students into learning. It's not needed every lesson, as we all have our bad days, but a good story is often enough to secure the minds of even the most challenging. It's all about connecting on the same level. After all, that is what makes teaching, teaching. Our life experiences can enrich our classrooms and that should *never* be ignored.

Linking a story to lesson content

However, it's essential to have a clear rationale about how the story you want to tell will be used in class and how it links to your lesson content. Remember, this is not about finding exciting activities and building an entire lesson plan around them. As

I suggested in Section 2, Idea 1, p. 61, always start by thinking about the learning you want to take place in the lesson. Jot this down for some upcoming lessons in the table below, then note down some of your favourite films, books and/or personal experiences that might help bring this learning to life. In the third column, think about how your story might then link to any activities or resources you intend to use in the classroom to develop learning further. I've included an example for a design technology lesson to get you started.

Learning/curriculum content	Film/book/experience	Classroom suggestion
Example: Problem solving and mechanisms (design technology)	Example: *The Man Who Touched the Sky* (book)	Example: Making rockets

Show me a photo of your completed table on Twitter using the hashtag #MarkPlanTeach.

Engaging students with stories and real-life experiences doesn't need to be something that is done consistently across the school, but it could make everyone's job a lot easier, particularly if used in aspects of teaching that are common practice, for example as a flying start activity (see Section 2, Idea 6, p. 86). It can help the determined teacher capture the minds of the most challenging, as well as the most gifted, students in the class.

If you are using storytelling in your classroom, make sure you ask yourself the following:

- Do your lesson plans incorporate links to real-life experiences or examples?

- If so, do the links then feed into the resources you intend to use in the classroom?

- Is there a strong basis for planning? If so, how could storytelling be built into the initial lesson structure?

- If the scheme of learning is written by another teacher, how could you adapt the plans to suit your own personal experiences and the stories you have to tell?

Storytelling and literacy

If you can embed storytelling techniques into your lesson planning and delivery, then you are also promoting a love of reading, speaking and listening in the classroom. This is something that every teacher hopes to impart as part of their professional duties. The Literacy Trust has conducted research looking at levels of reading for enjoyment among children. Their findings show:

'... nearly 6 in 10 children [enjoy] reading. More girls than boys enjoy reading with the gap increasing with age. In general, younger pupils are more likely to enjoy reading than their older peers.' (Clark and Teravainen, 2017)

Reading enjoyment is connected to behaviour and motivation, so it's important to engage your students in the magic of stories and give them every opportunity to read aloud in class, so they become more confident and more avid readers. You might even find it reduces the amount of time they spend connected to digital devices.

There is extensive evidence in this area from a range of studies over the past thirty years. Below I have quoted the 'Reading Comprehension Strategies' summary from the EEF's Teaching and Learning Toolkit, which suggests that approaches to improve reading comprehension include:

'a range of techniques that enable pupils to comprehend the meaning of what is written, such as inferring the meaning from context, summarising or identifying key points, using graphic or semantic organisers, developing questioning strategies, and monitoring their own comprehension and identifying difficulties themselves.'

The summary goes on to report that several of these techniques can be 'usefully combined with phonics, collaborative and peer-learning techniques' (EEF, 2017d). It is therefore clear that, when carefully selected according to the needs of your students via lesson planning, telling stories in class can develop techniques of reading comprehension, all the while providing effective engagement and challenge in relation to the lesson content.

In this section, I have referred to storytelling. Dr Tim O'Brien once introduced me to the concept of a different type of story – one that people continually tell to themselves and that exists inside their head. He calls it an 'inner story'. Read on to find out more about why inner stories are so relevant to us as teachers.

Psychology and...
inner story

You have two stories inside your head. One is about your life. The other is controlling your life. I call the story that controls your life your inner story. You may want to read a book I have written about it (O'Brien, 2015). Your inner story is created in your mind and you are living it every moment of every day. It is an internally constructed narrative about what it means to be you. The more you tell yourself your inner story, the more you become that story. One way that people offer an insight into their inner story is when they start a sentence with 'I am the sort of person who…'. Please complete the sentence a few times and see what you notice.

As a teacher, when you interact with a young person, you are always interacting with their inner story and they are always interacting with yours. Your influence on their internal narrative is very powerful. What you say and do – and how you say and do it – makes a contribution to shaping who the young person thinks they are both as a person and as a learner.

In any mass education system, every learner's inner story is potentially at risk. This is particularly the case if the young person experiences learning difficulties in systems where deficit-focused labels abound. In such systems, 'the problem' is seen as being located within the child and therefore children who experience difficulties, especially those who experience SEND, are in danger of being treated as if they are broken washing machines that need fixing. However, the problem might not be the problem. The notion that the adults or the environment should change, in order to enable the young person to change, can often be absent from the agenda.

Inner stories do not have to be bad to get better. Think of any young person that you teach. How do your interactions with them contribute to shaping their inner story? What can you do to help change their inner story for the better? Think of a colleague and ask yourself the same questions. How about you? Is your inner story empowering you or is it holding you back? What could you think, feel or do differently to change your inner story for the better? Answer the question. Start now. Make a change.

– Dr Tim O'Brien

Stickability

IDEA 4

IDEA SNAPSHOT

Do your lessons have staying power? For the past ten years, I have been conscious of the term 'stickability' in my lesson planning. Since I discovered it, this word has transformed my classroom practice because my focus is now much more on learning and memory, rather than on students doing and forgetting. Stickability can be defined as:

1. What learning should 'stick' in the minds of students?

2. What key point(s) do you want students to remember and bring back to the next lesson?

This idea will show you how to integrate stickability into your lesson planning.

'**S**tickability', or 'sticking power', is a term used in the 5 Minute Lesson Plan (see Section 2, Introduction, p. 57). Such is its importance that 'Stickability' was even going to be the title for this book, but it didn't quite stick with the publishers! Teaching ideas that stick – or ideas backed by cognition and pragmatic application – is the same as setting students up with learning objectives. The only difference is that the focus is on the actual end goal and success criteria, not just on what we hope to achieve. By aiming for 'what learning should stick' when you teach a lesson, the focus of your planning will be to help students reach that goal, rather than on offering a haphazard hit-and-hope objective at the beginning of a lesson.

Living and dying by the ideology of stickability then, what one thing would I want you to take away from this book? Well, here goes:

When the shift in lesson planning moves away from *doing* in favour of *learning* and hones in on the key points students must take away with them, lesson planning becomes sharper. A greater commitment is made in your teaching to ensure students leave your classroom with what has been *learnt*, not what has been *done*.

Stickability is fundamentally what learning and lesson planning should be all about. With relation to lesson planning, stickability can be defined as the following:

1. What is the fundamental aspect of the lesson that you need students to learn?

2. What key skill, knowledge or understanding should students grasp?

3. What should students leave your classroom knowing or understanding? What should students return to class knowing or understanding?

4. Why should this skill, knowledge or understanding stick with students? And how will you make it stick?

5. How will you know that it has stuck? And if students become unstuck, then what?

There are clearly a lot of sticky questions to answer, so I will try to offer some guidance.

As we've seen in previous ideas in this section, good teaching focuses on the learning and not on the activity. This is fundamental; once we are clear about what learning we want to stick, lesson planning can remain loose and adaptable. A lesson without learning at its heart is rigid and has more emphasis on a fixed, detailed lesson plan and the activities students must complete.

From curriculum plan to lesson plan

If we don't require written lesson plans, but do consider planning in some form to be important, how can we enable curriculum plans to feed into day-to-day lesson planning without it becoming a burden on the teacher?

We should expect that long-term planning exists – although in my experience, you cannot always assume this to be true. It is always worth digging into schemes of work to see if they are current, relevant and are providing challenge and development for all student abilities. A PowerPoint is not a scheme of work, nor is a document or a project you have been teaching for over ten years.

Curriculum reform is happening in many of the 35 OECD countries and it's important that schools, teachers and subject departments are working within the latest guidance. There are benefits to curriculum reform. A paper by the OECD notes that 'changes in the educational system or in pedagogies can help customise the educational process'. However, curriculum reform is brought about in different ways across OECD countries:

> 'Out of 26 analysed education systems, 13 relied more on schools than on central level in bringing about curriculum innovations, while 8 out of 26 expected innovation to originate from centrally driven processes than from schools. Five OECD countries applied a mixed approach to curriculum innovation.' (OECD, 2014)

I would argue that teachers need curriculum autonomy at a local level and some freedom to interpret curriculum mapping into classroom resources for their students. Lesson planning should then stem from schemes of work that feed into short-term planning in a teacher's day-to-day lesson planner. The OECD report looks at the high levels of autonomy given to teachers in Finland in terms of the curriculum and accountability, and the report attributes this to the high levels of trust between teachers, school leaders, parents, students and the authorities (OECD, 2014).

Unfortunately, the level of autonomy granted to teachers when it comes to curriculum reform is out of the hands of most classroom teachers, but we can define how lesson planning looks. In my opinion, the journey from curriculum to scheme of work and from lesson objectives to goal setting can be simplified as stickability. Stickability is the end product. It is the cognitive aspect of lesson planning, namely working out how to build into our lessons the mental action or process of acquiring knowledge and understanding through thought, experience and the senses, and adapting elements of teaching plans based on the 'why?' test (see Section 2, Idea 2, p. 67). This is how we can improve autonomy for teachers, help to reduce workload and steer planning so it zooms in on learning.

I hope by now you will agree that there is no point in planning if we are not focused on learning and are simply producing reams and reams of lesson plans for evidence-mongers. Schools should not expect teachers to produce individual lesson plans for observed or unobserved lessons, but sadly this is not the case in many of our schools, and it is partially to blame for the teacher workload crisis we are currently experiencing in England.

Two of the five secondary schools in which I have worked did not expect teachers to produce individual lesson plans, but did expect 'evidence of planning' over time. The need for detail was removed and replaced with an overview, and the teacher planner could contain the difference between the scheme of work and the lesson a teacher intends to teach. More importantly, trusting that teachers were considering the 'why?' of their teaching and what must stick in lessons was the *ordre du jour*. The impact? Well, surely it's obvious (depending on whose side you're on…).

The 5 Minute Lesson Plan (see Section 2, Introduction, p. 57) is a useful tool for recording the thinking behind a lesson plan on one page, removing the need for laboriously writing lengthy notes. It's perfect for teachers who may wish to plan or for those who still need to develop their planning in order to teach more confidently.

Collegial support

When it comes to lesson planning, collegial support (collaboration between teachers, schools and other providers) is essential. Here are some findings from research by the Teacher Development Trust:

> 'Where using collaborative approaches, providers and schools should allow participants to engage in collegial problem solving approaches that are focussed on improving student outcomes. Both parties should also consider how to embed broader processes across a school, to sustain opportunities for collaborative engagement with content and co-planning to address specific pupil learning needs.' (Teacher Development Trust, 2014)

As part of my role as a school leader of professional development, I facilitated teachers to work in paired departments to review lesson planning as part of teaching and learning policy implementation. Each department was paired with another and they were provided with resources to facilitate planning as a whole – from curriculum plans and schemes of work, right down to the teacher planner.

The impact of this collaboration on lesson planning is clear:

- It allows progress against whole-school thinking to be reviewed.

- It provides teachers with opportunities to think about best practice and to share their ideas with others.

- It enables teachers to review how the curriculum feeds into schemes of work and lesson planning, and how overarching plans feed into their colleagues' individual teacher planners.

If you were able to introduce a similar collaborative approach to lesson planning in your school, it would be the perfect opportunity to explore how stickability could work for you and your colleagues.

Making learning stick

In *Make It Stick*, Peter Brown, Henry Roediger III and Mark McDaniel remind us, 'the most successful learners are those who take charge of their own learning and follow a simple but disciplined strategy' (Brown et al., 2014). The issue for teachers is that we are so bombarded with external pressures to achieve X number of grades and levels of progress, that curriculum coverage leaves us with very little time to teach students how to be disciplined or how to learn and revise.

Teaching students how to make learning stick is essential and we should make the teaching of study strategies a habit, allocating them structured time in our lesson plans and pursuing them regularly. As Brown et al. (2014) suggest, we should:

'Embrace the fact that significant learning is often, or even usually, somewhat difficult […] These are signs of effort, not failure.'

We should be encouraging and promoting this growth mindset (see Section 1, Idea 2, p. 13) among all our students. If we can achieve this, making learning stick lies within our control.

EVIDENCE

Making learning stick can, of course, be considered at all levels – marking, planning and teaching – but in terms of planning, a technique called practice retrieval is recommended and is supported by evidence and research. Practice retrieval means quizzing yourself from memory on information you have just read or listened to and it can be used as a primary study strategy.

So, how can teachers incorporate this into their lesson planning? Well, we must coach students on how to study. This might seem quite simple to you and me, but it's not so clear for the students we teach. The following is a concise version of the information retrieval model suggested by Brown, Roediger III and McDaniel in *Make It Stick*:

CONTINUES OVER PAGE

1. Read a text.

2. Pause.

3. Ask questions.

4. Quiz yourself.

5. Write down the answers.

6. Set time aside to revisit the content and quiz yourself again. (Brown et al., 2014)

Introducing a pause in-between reading the text and testing yourself on it is a form of 'spaced practice'. Cognitive psychological scientists Yana Weinstein and Megan Smith of The Learning Scientists blog define spaced practice as:

> 'the exact opposite of cramming. When you cram, you study for a long, intense period of time close to an exam. When you space your learning, you take that same amount of study time, and spread it out across a much longer period of time.' (Weinstein and Smith, 2016)

Spaced practice can also involve gradually intertwining various topics to force the learner to recap on past knowledge in-between learning new information. We saw the importance of recapping on knowledge with the Ebbinghaus Forgetting Curve in Section 1, Idea 6, p. 34. Interleaving topics means placing wider gaps between learning the content and repeating the content, and as Alex Quigley says in *The Confident Teacher*, 'the brain is forced to do a harder job at remembering' (Quigley, 2016).

So, now we know a simple method for retaining information, how can teachers weave this into their lesson plans to help make learning stick and to stop students leaving revision to the last minute? Here lies the challenge, particularly when curriculum coverage and time pressures ensue.

As teachers, it's important that we give students opportunities to retrieve and elaborate on their studies by building time for recall into schemes of work, while also taking into account curriculum and syllabus coverage. If this is left as a bolt-on, it can make day-to-day teaching and learning difficult for all. Secondary teachers can use the fact that they teach in block periods, often separated out by several days, to plan lessons in a sequence that balances learning new content with recapping to consolidate prior learning.

Every teacher must discover what works in their classroom. The subject and age group will determine what is taught and what must be retaught, but there is one aspect of making learning stick that is essential in all settings, namely explaining to students how learning works. This is often left to the latter years of school life when examinations are pending but by then, bad habits will already have formed. We must instil in our students the importance of information retrieval throughout their education with careful curriculum design and lesson planning. It is a key strategy to help improve memory and learning.

The struggle zone

IDEA SNAPSHOT

When planning lessons, it is vital for teachers to keep in mind the 'struggle zone', namely the point at which students feel challenged and can push themselves to the limits of their knowledge and understanding. This is essential for teachers who want to differentiate to ensure that their teaching has a high impact for students of all abilities.

I n *Making Every Lesson Count*, Deputy Headteacher Shaun Allison and co-author Andy Tharby of Durrington High School in West Sussex have formulated a very popular teaching approach based on six principles: 'challenge', 'explanation', 'modelling', 'deliberate practice', 'questioning' and 'feedback' (Allison and Tharby, 2015). These principles inform their school's teaching and learning policy. I would recommend using this approach specifically when lesson planning and when assessing students' progress.

Allison and Tharby believe that 'expert teaching requires challenge so that students have high expectations of what they can achieve'. When it comes to planning, it is therefore essential for teachers to include some form of struggle or challenge. Keeping students in the struggle zone means walking the fine line between students becoming apathetic due to boredom and students giving up because of stress or a feeling that they are incapable. Allison and Tharby see the struggle zone as sitting in-between the 'comfort zone' and the 'panic zone'. They describe it as 'High challenge. Low stress. Thinking required. Effective learning.' (Allison and Tharby, 2015)

So how can a teacher plan to provide high challenge but low stress? How can they require students to think hard in order to achieve effective learning? Well, it's a tough ask for any teacher and it's even tougher to do every lesson.

First and foremost, teachers must consider the comfort and panic zones of all students in their lesson. It is of course vital that teachers know their students and they can do so through the relationships they have with them and the current data they have available. However, another way of knowing where students are going and when they are struggling or bored is through assessment, such as questioning. Assessment is all about challenge, pitch and delivery. Knowing how to use assessment to guide students and help them to improve without causing them anxiety is something every teacher must learn.

Planning for assessment

Planned questioning is rarely discussed in teacher training sessions and lack of development in this area can lead to teachers not knowing how to assess student progress on the spur of the moment. Dylan Wiliam and Paul Black, both Emeritus Professors at the UCL Institute of Education, have written a short, yet revered, document on assessment: *Inside the Black Box: Raising Standards through Classroom Assessment*. It's a powerful read – who says great things don't come in small packages? Wiliam and Black warn us that:

> 'There is a wealth of research evidence that the everyday practice of assessment in classrooms is beset with problems and shortcomings […] For primary teachers particularly, there is a tendency to emphasize quantity and presentation of work and to neglect its quality in relation to learning.' (Black and Wiliam, 2001)

In my experience, this applies to secondary teaching too and is perhaps an indication of how education has lost its way and has become a victim of evidence trails and accountability on a grand scale. Teachers have lost sight of what it is they are supposed to be doing with children because they have become so fixated on *what others think* of what they are doing.

Many schools no longer require lesson plans but do want to see evidence of planning. I would go one step further and declare that there should be no expectation on teachers to provide lesson plans for any observations either. This will help teachers manage their workload. Of course, this is not to undermine the need for planning full stop or for the newly qualified teacher – or the experienced soul who has just changed schools – who needs to use existing curriculum plans and lesson planning frameworks to help settle into a new way of working. But whether we write lesson plans or not, how do we know where students are going? Planning for assessment could be one of several ways. As Allison and Tharby say:

> '[Assessment] also helps to shift your view of students – rather than thinking about them as low ability, think of them as having a low starting point.' (Allison and Tharby, 2015)

So, when planning to keep all students in the struggle zone, ask yourself:

- How do you assess where your students are at during the lesson?
- Do you know where you want them to go?
- What teaching strategies are you going to use?
- What key questions will help you to lure students into learning?
- What classroom strategies will you use to keep students on task, motivated and working to their potential?

A careful plan that takes into account all the above can make a significant difference in helping you to deliver a perfectly pitched lesson that meets the needs of all students. It's difficult, but not impossible to achieve.

Psychology and...
The Zone of Proximal Development

Ross referring to a zone that promotes learning prompts me to discuss the Vygotskian concept of 'The Zone of Proximal Development' (ZPD). Lev Vygotsky, a Russian psychologist, was particularly interested in how human learning potential is socially mediated. I shall characterise his view as: learning takes place better between two or more heads than it does inside one. Vygotsky asserts that an important index of a person's learning and development is not their actual level – where they are right now – but their potential level. He describes the difference or distance between a learner's actual level and their potential level as the ZPD.

The teacher should teach within the ZPD, aware that a learner's processes are in a state of developing maturation. To help learners move through the ZPD, a teacher must believe the learner has the potential to be different. The learner needs to interact with supportive people, who assist learning by knowing what the learner does not currently know and enabling cognitive apprenticeship. On most occasions, that supportive other is a teacher. The teacher needs to have a notional idea of the actual level of the learner, be clear about where they want the learner to go in terms of a potential level and develop a plan of best interactions, including scaffolding, that will enable a learner's potential to be realised. Scaffolding does tend to be conceptualised as a one-way process but it is also possible for it to be negotiated between teacher and learner.

I suggest that a deepening awareness of metacognition, by the teacher and the learner, is a valuable component of scaffolding within the ZPD. In 1979, John Flavell, a developmental psychologist, coined the term 'metacognition'. It referred to the knowledge a person has about their own cognition in relation to learning processes. Metacognition, a higher order activity associated with self-regulation, enables us to, for example, learn about learning or think about thinking. Some researchers believe this to be a deliberately conscious process, whilst others assert that metacognition involves unconscious processes too. I recommend that specific opportunities to focus and reflect on metacognition be built in when teachers are planning. It offers teachers insight into a learner's ZPD. It also enables students to learn about how they learn and become more resilient when approaching and encountering cognitive and emotional challenge within their own ZPD.

– Dr Tim O'Brien

A flying start

IDEA SNAPSHOT

How can we get lessons off to a flying start without an onerous expectation on teachers to spend hours planning complex activities that may or may not have an impact on learning? In this idea, we'll look at a range of simple flying starts that genuinely impact learning, take minimal time to prepare and focus on the importance of literacy.

flying start to a lesson engages students from the outset and will help build up to the main parts of the lesson and the challenges that lie ahead. A flying start can also provide an opportunity to remind students of classroom expectations and routines. If tasks are established time and time again, students will know what is expected of them as soon as they arrive in your classroom. They will become accustomed to your expectations and be quicker to respond to them. This will help you to manage behaviour and set the tone for the lesson to ensure optimum conditions for learning. On the whole, students will participate no matter what the teacher asks them to do because this will be the norm, even when the teacher takes risks.

Simple flying starts have the greatest impact. I would recommend routines, one-off performances and simple strategies to recap on the previous lesson and introduce what's coming up. Unusual and unpredictable resources can often hold the most interest, as well as current affairs and news stories. Of course, teachers reading this book will most likely be equipped with numerous ready-made starter activities and strategies to deploy with any class, but here's my two pennies' worth in this idea.

Meet and greet

Flying starts can include meeting and greeting students at the door as they enter the classroom. The teacher welcomes the students one by one and asks them to sit down and work independently while the remaining students arrive. The students could be asked to get on with work put in front of them or consolidate information from the previous lesson, so they understand that this lesson is a continuation of the last. You could also ask them to complete a redrafting exercise, such as the 'yellow box' technique. See Section 1, Idea 3, p. 17 for more on this.

Stickability

Use techniques to break down the learning objectives or what learning you want 'to stick'. See Section 2, Idea 4, p. 78 for more on this.

Technology

Simple pieces of software, such as SMS Generator (just one of thousands of examples), provide teachers with the tools to write and share their own news stories and to encourage students to step into the shoes of a famous person and write some history of their own. This is a perfect tool for a flying start. It helps students develop creative writing skills and raises the profile of literacy. It also provides you with the opportunity to teach students how to decipher what is and what isn't real news, which is essential today given the plethora of social media channels that generate and share 'fake news'.

SMS Generator comes from the excellent website www.classtools.net, created by Russel Tarr, currently Head of History at the International School of Toulouse, France. The website enables you to create your own activities, games, quizzes and diagrams in minutes. Use them at the beginning of your lesson to get it off to a flying start and engage students in their learning.

Keywords

When it comes to lesson planning, teachers should *stop* planning to teach several keywords in every lesson, unless it is, for example, a French revision class, which requires students to build up their vocabulary. Forget trying to teach keywords by writing them all on the board for students to copy down. This may lead to complications and misconceptions. It also makes what you are trying to teach too generic and will reduce its impact.

Instead, I recommend that all teachers try teaching the etymology and root meaning of a keyword. Break the word down into parts so that students not only understand how to spell the keyword but acquire a secure grasp of its meaning and origin throughout history. And this is not just for teachers of English. I find it fascinating that even when teaching in your own subject, there is a whole new world waiting to be discovered when breaking keywords down into more refined details.

You could also try the 'snowball' technique to recap keywords at the beginning of a lesson. Ask students to spell three words of your choice on a piece of paper. They then scrunch the paper up into a snowball and throw it across the room. Students find one of the snowballs, open it up, spell check the words written on it and write down three more keywords of your choice. The snowballs are then thrown a second time. You can do this as many times as you like, with as many keywords as you want, but I usually stick to ten.

Reducing the number of words to recall can support the long-term memory. Teachers can therefore start to use more difficult words and concepts with younger students. Even better, if this strategy becomes a routine, then students are likely to use keywords in their speaking, listening, reading and writing activities in class.

The importance of literacy

Several of my ideas for an effective flying start to a lesson relate to literacy. I believe that literacy should feature heavily in our lessons, so why not start as you mean to go on and introduce it right at the beginning of class? Literacy is central to teaching across the curriculum. According to the Teachers' Standards for England (DfE, 2011), a teacher must:

> 'demonstrate an understanding of and take responsibility for promoting high standards of literacy, articulacy and the correct use of standard English, whatever the teacher's specialist subject.'

Every classroom teacher should take a moment to think about how assessment in their subject links to literacy and how they are currently embedding literacy in their lesson plans. What do you already do and what's missing? Use the following questions to reflect on and start to identify how you could develop your teaching of literacy further. I know there are many areas where I could improve...

1. Why is literacy central to teaching?

2. Why should learning and literacy be considered very closely related?

3. Why is learning that takes no account of literacy never going to be better than poor teaching?

4. What role can language play in the development of children's learning?

5. Why might specialist language be critical to securing a teacher's long-term subject confidence?

6. How could literacy link to your subject?

7. How well do you know your students' literacy levels and reading ages?

8. Is there an expectation in your school that every child has a reading book?

9. Is there an expectation that every teacher shares what they are reading with their students?

10. What opportunities do you give for extended pieces of writing in your subject?

It is critical to support a student who is walking a fine line between failing and succeeding at literacy (particularly if they are a reluctant student), so they understand and see the potential benefits of dealing with these challenges. Every child knows they need to be able to read, but if students are reluctant, at what point should the teacher step up to support them and what can they do to help?

When it comes to literacy, role models are key, as are opportunities to be part of activities that enrich a student's life. Students take inspiration from great writers, poets and people from their communities – role models who provide a level of openness and expertise that most busy classroom teachers cannot offer. Students often express their feelings more freely with adults who are not their teachers. This can open many doors and can develop a student's confidence to speak out.

A great example of enrichment opportunities, in which I have seen children of 11 years of age with reading ages of six or seven, read out loud in front of 200 peers, is the wonderful work of Humanutopia. They provide workshops, assemblies and classes that aim to have a positive effect on the 'hope, confidence, happiness, relationships and employability of young people' (Humanutopia, 2016). I have seen many members of staff wipe a tear from their eye when a reluctant student faces their fears through the inspirational work that Humanutopia are doing all over the UK. These are moments every school should embrace; they are, after all, the reason we do the job we love.

In her brilliant book *Cleverlands*, Lucy Crehan reminds us that Finland has one of the highest literacy rates in the world, but 'this doesn't rule out the possibility that their late school start has a negative influence on children's later reading skills' (Crehan, 2016).

Of all the various opinions about teaching and learning, there is one common thread that all educators will agree on, namely that literacy is the one thing that has the greatest impact on learning. A student's level of language, fluency and love for reading will have a significant bearing on their overall attainment. Without a good level of literacy, students are unable to access learning in a large variety of circumstances in the classroom. If additional effort is needed to decode text while reading in class or independently, access to learning will be more challenging for the student and for the teacher.

For many years, I've used Accelerated Reader, a tool by Renaissance Learning that monitors independent reading among children and young people, to improve my students' reading confidence and engagement. Research by the National Literacy Trust and Coventry University questioned whether students 'who use Accelerated Reader (AR) think differently about reading', whether 'they enjoy reading more' and whether 'they do it more often than [those] who do not use AR'. The findings were conclusive:

- 58.8% of students who use AR 'enjoy reading either very much or quite a lot', compared with 51.9% of students who do not use AR.

- More students using AR 'read frequently outside class' compared with students not using AR.

- Students using AR think more positively about reading; 48.5% of AR students 'think that reading is cool' compared to 37.5% of non-AR students. (Clark and Cunningham, 2016)

CONTINUES OVER PAGE

This research shows that interventions to boost reading enjoyment can work and underlines the value of developing effective teaching methods to encourage students to read for pleasure. This will come as no surprise to teachers. We know a love of reading is of paramount importance in school and at home, and that there are things we can do to create a reading culture across our schools. However, the greatest challenge for us all is ensuring this reading culture reaches the homes of our most disadvantaged students.

It would be my recommendation to every teacher wanting to improve reading engagement and reading age, as well as students' understanding of subject knowledge, to commence all lessons with a flying start. No matter what this task looks like, ensure that literacy features heavily and that you keep all students in mind – from the most vulnerable to the most able – when you plan it.

Quality first teaching

IDEA SNAPSHOT

The quality of teaching in the classroom has the single greatest impact on student outcomes when compared to any other intervention. 'Quality first' teaching is exactly what it says: quality teaching that is utilised to its full potential before any other intervention is considered. Of course, if specific learning needs are identified, a teacher should seek interventions elsewhere, but only if all else fails or if additional support from EAL teachers or the special needs department, for example, is being provided. To achieve quality first teaching, appropriate differentiation in class is essential and in this idea, I will explore how we can plan lessons that help *all* learners achieve their potential.

High-quality teaching should always be considered the first wave of intervention. Research from the Education Development Trust (EDT) suggests:

'Teachers are one of the key elements in any school and effective teaching is one of the key propellers for school improvement.' (Ko et al., 2014)

It is therefore paramount that we invest in our teachers and give them the time they need to develop their practice and achieve their goals. We need our teachers to be research informed, so they can:

- be clear on lesson objectives and communicate these to students across a range of abilities

- become knowledgeable about curriculum content

- make use of available resources to support learning

- teach cognitive strategies to their students to support their learning

- provide appropriate and timely feedback.

For any school, part and parcel of this challenge is ensuring there is consistency in all classrooms. If every teacher adopts all of the above except for Mr McGill in the classroom next door to you, who is long in the tooth, believes he has 'seen it all before' and 'just wants to teach', the entire school will still have a problem.

It's important that schools establish consistency in their approach to quality first teaching and as the EDT suggest, 'engender a culture of professional debate and developmental lesson observation' (Ko et al., 2014). Quality first teaching can only be achieved in a culture of trust. Sadly, this is hard to find in some of the more challenging schools we teach in today. The external machine drives schools to regularly monitor and evaluate what they are doing and although this is apparently a voluntary stipulation, they are punished for lack of leadership, direction and evidence of improvement if they fail to provide reams of evidence and data. This pressure to perform and always be improving filters down to individual teachers and students. It's not possible for all students to achieve the best grades in the current English examination system because allocation of grades is distributed. So peddling myths that *all* students can achieve the top grade is simply unhelpful.

As former secondary headteacher, Tom Sherrington, writes in his blog post 'The Bell-Curve Cage: Something Must Break', the problem with external accountability on schools and teachers is:

> 'If you're using the same mechanisms – i.e. our national examinations – to measure both improvement and standards, you're stuffed. You can't keep a firm hold on standards with a bell curve cage and, simultaneously, proclaim improvement.' (Sherrington, 2017)

Sherrington adds that this 'pressure to improve' is a 'head-on car-crash collision' waiting to happen because 'everyone must improve but not everyone is allowed to'. These external pressures reach all the way down to every child and their performance.

For the past ten years, I have worked in difficult schools with some of the most disadvantaged children in this country. To achieve a degree of consistency with over one hundred teachers in any of these schools is a huge challenge. The priority has always been the child, but often what precedes the needs of the child is the quality of teaching in each individual classroom. How do schools achieve consistency when working in challenging environments? I do not have the answer to this in the current climate, but what I do know is that it is vital for all teachers to approach quality first teaching as a differentiation strategy and one that will be delivered over time, not as a one-off, quick-fix solution.

Quality first teaching and differentiation

So, with the needs of your own students in mind, how can you plan for differentiation to ensure quality first teaching?

Differentiation is not a one-off exercise. You should not be overexerting yourself with endless planning for individual lessons, especially for something that is incredibly challenging to achieve and often completely unrealistic to attain. This is neither effective nor sustainable and has a wholly negative impact on workload and productivity.

Differentiation should be planned over time to ensure a quality first approach that meets the needs of all students and maximises the use of any additional adults in the room. Taking a graduated approach to differentiation and ensuring quality first teaching for all students are both embedded in the SEND Code of Practice for England (DfE, 2014b). The most useful form of differentiation is marking students' books and using this marking to adapt lesson plans to the needs of individual students and groups in your class. In staff self-reviews, however, I have found this is often cited as the most challenging aspect of teaching.

So, what else could we be doing to differentiate our lessons over time? Below are a few suggestions.

Conversations

Give yourself time to speak with students and colleagues outside of lessons. It never ceases to amaze me what a brief conversation with a student in the playground, just before a lesson, can achieve. Checking in with students to discuss the expectations you have when they first arrive in your classroom can have a huge impact, especially if there is an issue that needs to be resolved from the previous lesson.

Modelling writing

For students who struggle with language, modelling written tasks, by completing them alongside the student, can be hugely beneficial. This is the most obvious idea, but one that's difficult to achieve with 29 other students in the classroom. A solution is displaying work via a video link, enabling all students to see you doing the work alongside them as a teacher. I'd guess that if you are doing it too, the students will be more likely to value the work and invest in the activity or task being asked of them.

Scaffolding oracy and writing frames

Scaffolding oracy and providing writing frames for students of varying abilities can embed learning at all levels over a period of time. This can support students of all abilities and allow them to work independently, freeing you up to assist individual students. Where possible, you can also systematically check understanding in the lesson through self- and peer-assessment techniques (see Section 1, Idea 9, p. 45).

EAL students

Following the advice of Dr Jim Cummins, the cognitive challenge of some tasks will need to be lowered when students are new to English and are learning a lot of new vocabulary. This doesn't mean we should lower our expectations, but it is certainly something we should consider when teaching a large number of students with EAL. Cummins suggests that we can keep cognitive challenge high for EAL learners, if we provide students with **context**. This could be through visual hand signals or facial expressions, graphics or collaborative opportunities that allow EAL students to work with peers.

To support EAL learners further, we should consider using culturally accessible materials to help them sequence learning. If you're lucky enough to have a specialist in your school, you could also ask them to translate a text into the students' home language, so students can – with dictionary in hand – highlight keywords with you and practise extrapolating the spelling and meaning of these words in English.

Seating plans

To differentiate successfully, you must build a seating plan that takes into account students' starting points and pathways. I would advocate the use of seating plans in every classroom. They provide stability, ensure students know who is in control and mean that every learner will be working in a place where they can be supported and challenged most effectively. Seating plans are really the easiest solution for differentiation and I'm always surprised at how many teachers fail to use such a simple strategy for quality first teaching.

Seating plans have many advantages:

- They can be seen as evidence that a teacher has processed the data available for the class.

- They help establish authority over a new class. Where students sit should always be up to the teacher. 'We always work better when we sit together, Sir/Miss' is most frequently an indication that they do not!

- Changing the seating plan at the start of every term is easy and the new dynamics keep things fresh.

- A boy–girl seating plan rarely fails, difficult though it can be to implement in the more boy- or girl-heavy year groups.

- They can be easily accessed by another member of staff, who you may need to help with the class, such as a pastoral leader or your head of department.

- They can show you things you may have inadvertently missed, such as whether all your Pupil Premium students are sitting together at the back or where a gifted and talented student, who wants you to forget about their high prior attainment, is sitting.

- You could consider having a 'home' and 'away' arrangement, with 'away' being an alternative seating plan you use from time to time, for example when you want students to work in groups not based on where they usually sit.

Creating a supportive environment

No matter which differentiation strategies you decide to use, to provide quality first teaching over time, you will also need to use techniques to help create a supportive and inclusive classroom environment for all students, regardless of ability and background. Ask yourself the following questions to ensure you are including techniques in your lesson planning to allow all students to access subject knowledge across the curriculum and to support their language and literacy development:

1. Do you encourage and seek opportunities to use first language at the initial stage of learning?

2. Do you model and encourage an atmosphere of risk-taking where errors are seen as a natural part of learning (see Section 1, Idea 5, p. 29)?

3. Do you create opportunities to engage with new arrivals in the classroom, including early-stage EAL students or students with SEND?

4. Do you consciously interact with learners who do not speak English in your classroom?

5. Do you support your students to make links and build on previous learning and experiences?

6. Do you provide thinking and rehearsal time before students must speak up in front of the class?

7. Do you regularly monitor student understanding and allow opportunities for individual explanation?

8. Do you use visuals and identify keywords for clarity in your lessons?

9. Do you explicitly teach the subject-specific vocabulary?

10. Do you clarify keywords, provide synonyms, and rephrase key content in a variety of ways?

11. Do you use group work effectively for students to complete purposeful, cognitively demanding tasks?

12. If receiving EAL specialist support in lessons, do you plan your teaching tasks collaboratively?

13. Is your EAL specialist actively engaged in target setting for targeted EAL students?

14. Do you delegate the differentiation of your teaching and learning resources to your EAL specialist?

15. Have you found EAL CPD opportunities an effective way to improve your teaching practice? If not, what could they do to make a difference?

By differentiating successfully and creating a supportive and inclusive classroom environment through planning, you will be providing your students with quality first teaching that will help all learners achieve their potential.

EVIDENCE

In this Evidence section, I have decided to examine one significant piece of research that considers an issue that prevails in schools everywhere: how best to use a second adult in the classroom.

In spring 2015, the EEF published 'Making Best Use of Teaching Assistants', a research report that sought to establish why teaching assistants (TAs) were 'not being used in ways that improve pupil outcomes'. The report made seven excellent evidence-based recommendations to help schools maximise the impact of TAs. Read the headlines below and think about what you could do differently when working with TAs to enable effective differentiation and provide quality first teaching in your classroom.

1. 'TAs should not be used as an informal teaching resource for low-attaining pupils.'

2. Teachers should 'use TAs to add value to what teachers do, not replace them'.

3. We should 'use TAs to help pupils develop independent learning skills and manage their own learning'.

4. Teachers should 'ensure TAs are fully prepared for their role in the classroom'.

5. TAs should be used 'to deliver high-quality one-to-one small group support using structured interventions'.

6. Schools should 'adopt evidence-based interventions to support TAs in their small group and one-to-one instruction'.

7. We should all 'ensure explicit connections are made between learning from everyday classroom teaching and structured interventions'. (Sharples et al., 2015)

NOTE: The first four points are recommended when using TAs in everyday classroom contexts; points five and six are for TAs delivering structured interventions out of class; and point seven is recommended for linking learning led by teachers and learning led by TAs.

In my experience in secondary schools, the fourth point above is the most challenging to achieve. The nature of school timetables, funding and teacher allocation all limit the amount of time a TA and teacher have to plan together. Often, schools deploy TAs to one particular student. This does ensure consistency for the student but often to the detriment of teacher–TA consistency, meaning the student is receiving support but often with a different adult to the one who is teaching them. I would accept that this issue is far less critical in primary school settings.

Inspiration

IDEA SNAPSHOT

We are all so bombarded with hogwash from inside and outside of our schools that we often take risks and teach 'off the cuff'. It is simply impossible to plan every lesson out in minute detail and even when we do, not everything will go according to plan 100% of the time. In this idea, I will look at how you can stockpile resources and strategies to help when things don't quite work out and your only option is to improvise.

We have all walked into a class hoping to wing our way through the hour ahead, usually because we are so stretched for time. And even if we do plan our lesson out meticulously beforehand, there is no guarantee that it won't fail miserably nonetheless. Every teacher will be able to recall a lesson that did not go according to plan – Johnny vomited all over the floor or Mariam and Ahmed got themselves into a tizz and started to 'cuss' each other across the classroom. You name it, we've all experienced the highs and lows of kids dominating proceedings between our four walls. At times, the reasons can be out of our control. On other occasions, they could have been prevented by simple teacher presence (either physical or verbal) to diffuse the situation before it erupted (though hindsight is a wonderful thing). As our experience grows, we are often pleasantly surprised that we have mastered the art of teaching on instinct, but how we do this is usually a mystery to our newly qualified colleagues.

So how do teachers plan for those moments when something goes wrong? Those situations where technology lets us down or a resource does not quite match the ability of those sitting in front of us? We've all been there, but what can we do to support ourselves the moment something exasperates us?

Stockpiling ideas

In the world of teaching, lesson planning happens everywhere, all the time, to help counteract these unplanned scenarios. Experienced teachers will know that planning can take place when you are totally relaxed in the bath on a Sunday night or overseas on holiday and then an idea just pops into your head. For instance, at a market stall on a sandy beach in Sri Lanka, you find a sari that would be perfect for a tie-dye project with your Year 8 students next year. And there you go. You are teaching 24/7, using your own experiences, your own time and (sadly) often your own cash to inspire your lesson planning. We magpie ideas left, right and centre to ensure we cover all bases. It's the nature of the role and our profession.

Here are some examples of how you can recognise that you're doing this and that you'll always have a plan B in case you ever need it:

1. Eating Jaffa Cakes always reminds you of that teacher on the advert, famous for teaching her children about the different phases of the moon as she stuffs the biscuit into her mouth. As you reminisce at the end of an exhausting week, you wonder what you could do with Penguin biscuits as you munch through a whole packet on the sofa.

2. You get excited by the new hole punch you've bought for your home office. So much so, you decide that it would make a perfect case study for product analysis and you pop it into your bag for a lesson later that day.

3. Your fancy dress outfit for that thirtieth birthday party on Saturday would also make a perfect costume for World Book Day and it's a great excuse for being in character in all your lessons.

4. Your family buy you a box of fifty highlighter pens for Christmas. Your body language indicates just how excited you are about the impact they will have on self-assessment and workload reduction in your lessons. Your family look on bemused.

Time-filler strategies

Stockpiling ideas is essential in case you ever have any unexpected spare time to fill in lessons. This could be caused by a simple lapse in concentration on your part or a break in routine, such as a collapsed timetable caused by external events – snow or an early closure for an open evening, for example.

I recall a time as a middle leader when I misread the clock on the classroom wall and finished a lesson too early. Once I realised, I ran out into the corridor, shouting for the students to return to class. You can just imagine how happy they all were. So, with chaos a distinct possibility, I was left in a predicament. I could either unpack all of the materials, machines and pieces of equipment for a practical task or use the last ten minutes to evaluate what we'd learnt in the lesson.

It was at that moment I realised I needed a bank of time-filler ideas for lessons that finish a wee bit early. Here are some of the best.

Five-minute time-filler strategies

These ideas are generic strategies that can be adapted to fill five minutes at any time in class:

- Discuss a topic from today's news and how this links to the learning.
- If you were the teacher, what would you do to ensure [insert student name] secures a higher grade?

- A game of Mastermind: 'And your specialist subject is…?'

- Make the teacher say 'yes' or 'no' based on the lesson content.

This list is endless and often, the more unusual the idea, the better!

Lesson-related ideas

The following are ideas that can be used to fill time at the end of class to recap on lesson content:

- The flying aeroplane technique: split the class into two groups and ask the groups to stand on opposite sides of the room; each group writes what they have learnt today on a paper plane; the students then throw the paper planes to each other; the students catch the planes, open them and read what's written on them, then fly them back. Chaos, but a real attention grabber.

- Recap on the learning: create a quick keyword spelling test or a subject quiz; offer prizes to the winner to ensure instant engagement and to make sure no one notices that you're improvising.

- Provide references for the next lesson: ask students to write their own learning objectives for the next lesson in groups; this must include an extended learning objective with challenge; offer a positive phone call home to the student who plans your next lesson.

- Discussion: draw students into a discussion about what they will be studying next week, next term or next year.

- Closed questions (agree or disagree/yes or no): ask closed questions and get students to move to different areas of the classroom to indicate their answers; refer back to phases of the lesson and lesson objectives.

Now you've heard mine, why not create your own list of last-minute time-filler strategies, so you can pull ideas out of the hat to suit the context of your lesson? Share it with me using the hashtag #MarkPlanTeach.

Time-filler strategies	
1.	2.
3.	4.
5.	6.
7.	8.
9.	10.

This forward planning will have you ready for any future car crash moment.

EVIDENCE

Teachers draw on sources of inspiration from every aspect of their lives. They would be unable to do their jobs without thinking creatively. Teaching is a non-stop mental activity with ideas for the classroom pouring into the mind when we least expect it. No wonder teachers find it difficult to switch off!

In the abstract of 'On Teaching Inspiration', Wang Liusheng says:

> 'Teaching inspiration will be aroused if teachers firmly pursue in their specialities, love and understand their students, and if they have a fine mood and are able to do the long-time arduous creative work.' (Wang, 2004)

A fine mood? That's rare in the life of a teacher, but I am often alert to the moments when I feel most creative in the classroom. They usually arise when I am far away from it! In fact, I source my best ideas when I am well rested and at home or travelling, but feeling inspired. A takeaway menu results in a new homework resource. A one-page summary of shapes equates to one of the most popular lesson plan templates in the world (my 5 Minute Lesson Plan, see p. 58) – all developed outside of the classroom. Oh, the irony!

When teachers' spirits are high – or when their mental health is in good condition – teachers can get the best out of themselves and their students. It's not rocket science. Perhaps if we changed the desire for schools to work teachers to maximum capacity and we released teachers from marking, burdensome lesson planning and data micromanagement, we could open up teachers' creative faculties. By reducing the time teachers are required to spend on mindless paperwork, instead offering them more time to work collaboratively or to be off-site to find inspiration, we may produce the results we actually want: more effective teachers who are more efficient and achieve better results. It's not a new idea.

The nonsensical nature of backwards-then-forwards policymaking has made it impossible for schools and teachers to establish effective solutions. The aim of Headteachers' Roundtable – a non-party political headteachers' group established in England in 2012 and now operating as a think tank – is to 'provide a vehicle for people working in the profession to influence national education policymakers so that education policy is centred upon what is best for the learning of all children' (Headteachers' Roundtable, 2017). Wouldn't that be something? Let's take our teachers out of the classroom – to be inspired and to inform government policy. At the Sheffield Institute of Education in July 2016, Headteachers' Roundtable produced an 'Alternative Green Paper' informed by evidence from a range of sources and expert advice. There are pearls of wisdom in this paper and I believe that every teacher, school leader and politician should read it. Let's give our teachers the conditions that they need to be inspired. Even if it's simply allowing them out of their school to visit other colleagues and see things from a different perspective, it's a start.

All change please!

IDEA SNAPSHOT

In the previous Idea, I discussed how you could improvise should external events or mistiming put your lesson planning up the spout, but what if behaviour is the reason that your lessons flop time and time again? How can we adapt our lesson plans to deal with disruption in the classroom and how do we prepare for these last-minute changes?

Although poor lesson planning, classroom resources that fail to deliver and external events (such as extreme weather or a fire alarm) are all cited as common reasons for lessons to flop, behaviour is often one of the main issues that disrupts perfectly planned lessons. We've already seen that there are many factors involved in teachers delivering consistently good lessons and, once we have mastered them, positive relationships and well-planned lessons catering for the needs of all students will help us to trump potential bad behaviour. Nevertheless, even the best of us can hold our hands up and admit that factors outside of our classroom can arrive on our doorstep and quash everything we've worked so hard for.

A case study

I am reminded of an ex-student (let's call him Sean) and what it must have been like to be him in a classroom. He was finding life particularly difficult and was struggling to meet expectations. He had been excluded a few times for several misdemeanours. He was under-performing across the board and disliked school.

Imagine, just for one moment, that you are this 14-year-old student in a large secondary school, moving from lesson to lesson on the sound of the bell once an hour, every hour. On the sound of this klaxon, you are expected to stop learning French and then walk calmly along the corridors – past hundreds of other spotty, hormonal teenagers – and arrive on time, smart and ready to learn maths, for example, the moment you step foot across the classroom threshold.

How would you feel if I told you to put this book down right now, even if you were really enjoying it (though maybe you are not…!), and asked you to start reading on another, completely unrelated topic? What if I then said to you that you couldn't pick this book up again until the same time next week? You'd probably find it pretty frustrating.

Is this model for schooling what we expect education to look like in the next ten or twenty years? Is this how I see my son learning at school over the next decade, even though we understand the brain and cognition a little better than we used to in the nineteenth and twentieth centuries? I hope not. As David Price says in his book, *Open: How We'll Work, Live and Learn in the Future*, learners now 'find themselves in the driving seat' because with the growth of technology, they can choose what to learn and when to learn it. School is no longer the only option available and Price recommends that educators 'have to look at the way [students] learn outside' the classroom if they are to keep them engaged in the classroom. He says:

> 'We in the West want to be more like those in the East, who, in turn, want to be more like we in the West. We call for learning fit to meet the challenges of the 21st century, while recommending teaching methods belonging to the 19th century […] In short, we're really, really confused.' (Price, 2013)

This all makes me wonder if our current model of schooling needs a revamp – but that's for another book.

If we return to our student, Sean, he is bored in your lesson and fails to understand the learning taking place. I say this because I know it happens in my classroom. I also know that there is a colossal range of factors outside school that will determine the mood of a child. This, coupled with the pressure of performance and the high expectations on teachers, makes schooling a pressure cooker for Sean and students like him.

How much of this pressure could you soak up each day, if you were Sean? Even though school is a safe environment, the current curriculum and timetable are restrictive and failing to keep him engaged. Of course, there are things schools can offer, such as counselling, but these skills and services are often out of reach for classroom teachers and we fall back on various professional development resources and use what data and information we have about our students to do our absolute best to educate them.

I know that if I have just one unsavoury interaction, it affects me for the entire day. Sean is experiencing this four or five times a day, naturally becoming increasingly grumpy and frustrated, and quickly reaching tipping point, where one more incident will send him over the edge. It could quite easily be in your lesson that a comment from a peer will be just the thing that does it.

It will be at this stage of the process that anything *any* teacher says is simply white noise. The student fails to see clearly; the bigger picture is a blur; conversations are muffled and behaviour can become challenging. Any further reprimands become background noise. The student turns off.

After several of these instances, Sean's attendance and academic performance deteriorate. A specialist is required, but this is becoming increasingly difficult for schools in England to secure due to reducing budgets.

Interventions and lesson planning

So, as classroom teachers, what can we do when planning lessons to prevent behavioural issues in our classrooms? A teacher should have the flexibility when planning their lesson to choose the interventions that will work with their students. Let's take a look at some guidance from the Teachers' Standards in England. Teachers should:

- 'Know when and how to differentiate appropriately, using approaches which enable pupils to be taught effectively.'

- 'Have a secure understanding of how a range of factors can inhibit pupils' ability to learn, and how best to overcome these.'

- 'Demonstrate an awareness of the physical, social and intellectual development of children, and know how to adapt teaching to support pupils' education at different stages of development.'

- 'Have a clear understanding of the needs of all pupils, including those with special educational needs; those of high ability; those with English as an additional language; those with disabilities; and be able to use and evaluate distinctive teaching approaches to engage and support them.' (DfE, 2011)

I suggest that it is essential for all teachers to take the above guidance into account when they plan lessons. With effective differentiation and an understanding of every child in your class, you will be on your way to keeping your students engaged and therefore help to prevent boredom, frustration and ultimately, disruptive behaviour.

However, when behaviour problems do crop up in class (and they will, despite our best efforts), lesson planning often has to take a backseat. As part of our duties as teachers, we must safeguard every child. Being able to understand the motivation for an outburst in a lesson and having the capacity to intervene at a critical point takes a high level of confidence and usually requires you to think on the spot. It's difficult to be able to offer a one-size-fits-all solution. There will be a specific context for every student, involving a multitude of factors, and every child must be treated equally and as an individual. The vast majority of teachers I know support students to a very sophisticated level and are fully aware and capable of understanding the emotions of a child. This increases with experience, but we are not experts in dealing with mental health.

If all else fails, I would strongly recommend the following in the heat of the moment:

- Speak softly.

- Adopt non-threatening body language. Take a step back.

- Speak in private. Avoid further sanctions in front of the whole class.

- If another adult is engaging with the student and they continue to be abusive to you, leave the scene (if possible) or ask the other adult to take the student away for a quiet walk.

- Seek support and training within your school to help you work with students who need additional support.

Flexibility

It is also essential that schools change their attitude towards lesson planning and allow teachers to take back control. In *Flip the System*, a book that gathers research and views from experienced educationalists from around the world, Lori Nazareno quotes Margaret Wheatley (a management consultant who studies organisational behaviour) as saying:

> 'We know that the best way to create ownership is to have those responsible for implementation develop the plan for themselves [...] It simply doesn't work to ask people to sign on when they haven't been involved in the planning process.' (Wheatley in: Nazareno, 2015)

In every school, teachers must be involved in the professional dialogue around lesson planning. They should also be responsible for changes made to lesson length, frequency and format. After all, we are talking about a highly educated workforce and they deserve to be granted autonomy in the decision-making process. Sadly, this is often not the case. In some schools, particularly in England, where we are seeing an increase in multi-academy trusts in some regions, organisation-wide policies and templates are distributed and forced upon individual teachers in the name of raising standards of education or for compliance, consistency and accountability.

EVIDENCE

There is an increased call for evidence in teaching and a demand for teachers to be informed more reliably than ever before. Advances in neuroscience have resulted in the investigation of the mind (the software) being combined with the investigation of the brain (the hardware). This is a branch of psychology known as cognitive neuroscience.

I am no expert here, but I do wonder if teachers have always been interested in how the mind works. With a vested interest in learning, surely teachers have always wondered how we learn. I would be very curious to go back in time and discuss these questions with the teachers who taught me thirty years ago. At that time, there would have been far less material available to help the everyday classroom teacher work smarter and implement ideas similar to the evidence-informed strategies I have been suggesting in this book.

Cognitivism is a rejection of psychoanalytic approaches, which try to understand the mind in terms of myth, and of behaviourist approaches, which try to understand the mind in terms of behaviour only. Cognitive strategies are one type of approach that students can use in order to learn more successfully. For example, successful problem solving strategies require us to go beyond the information provided and engage in abstract thinking. This could also include organising new language, summarising meaning and using memory.

This demand for evidence never existed in my formative years as a teacher (roughly twenty years ago), nor did the notion of evidence ever cross my lips during that time. However, this is not to say that teachers should not now want

In stark contrast, Pasi Sahlberg explains what Finland has to offer:

'Flexibility is one of the key denominators of education and economic development in Finland. The Education system went through a major transformation in the early 1990s when most state regulations were abolished and pathways to education opportunities were dramatically increased. Similarly, private sector regulations were loosened and more flexible standards were introduced …' (Sahlberg, 2014)

Bearing in mind that Finland has one of the greatest and most successful education systems in the world, surely increased flexibility is something we must consider. Devolution of classroom accountability should be the new norm. We should be able to abandon our lesson plans without fear of reprisal, in order to provide on-the-spot support to students like Sean. We should be able to change the task we had planned for the class, in order for students to be able to work independently while we seek a quiet space in the corridor to help Sean deal with any emotional issues and offer counselling until additional support arrives. Wouldn't that be a climate all teachers would like to work in? It would certainly work for me and it would have an impact for Sean, too.

to use or access research to improve teaching. They should. But I hope there is not a danger of research-hungry educators accepting claims of what works in the classroom only if there is hard evidence to support them. And I also hope that we can still consider that a teacher knows best and what works in their classroom is a valid evidence base on which they can build effective teaching strategies and develop their practice.

I'd like to argue that teachers should still continue to do what works for them without the need for evidence. But this will come at a price. If teachers are told to do X, Y and Z by senior leadership teams because external agencies have suggested that this is what 'good teaching' looks like with no evidence to back them up, we will continue to find various classroom gimmicks being peddled at conferences and on the Internet. Teachers will continue to do all sorts of tricks and one-off performances to please observers, even though there is no evidence to suggest they actually have an impact on learning.

Nevertheless, something has to change. We must be able to trust our teachers to get on with the job they do best. And sometimes, just sometimes, this can be done without any evidence to inform best practice. Do we really need league tables? Do teachers really need lesson plans that run to several pages? If we do, I fear for the mental health of our next generation of teachers. If we are to create a system where teachers can continue to have autonomy in their classrooms, the current climate of testing, measuring and evidencing needs to be eradicated or at least reformed. We must avoid ideological templates at all costs because the students I've taught will have entirely different needs and a very different context when compared to students in other parts of London, England or the world. It is vital we allow our teachers to plan, mark and teach with freedom and flexibility.

Psychology and...
behaviour that is challenging

When I refer to 'challenging behaviour', I mean behaviour that provides a challenge to the teacher, the school ethos, to other students or to the student who is presenting the behaviour. Behaviour defined as challenging should lead teachers to find solutions that make a positive difference rather than become stuck in the psychological cul-de-sac of problematising 'negative' behaviours.

All behaviour is communication and behaviour that is challenging can communicate needs that are unresolved or unmet. Causation may be related to, for example, emotional distress or trauma. It is the function I shall focus on, as establishing the function can provide solution-focused responses. Let's consider four overarching reasons why people behave in a challenging way. The function of the behaviour might relate to one of these reasons or could lie in varying combinations of the four.

1. **Give me some attention:** People may behave in a challenging way to communicate a need for attention – whatever that attention may look like. For some, it does not matter if the attention they receive is positive or negative, as long as they are gaining attention of some description.

2. **Get me out of here:** Challenging behaviour might communicate a need to escape from a situation that a person does not want to be in. Whatever the reason, the desire to escape is communicated through behaviour.

3. **It feels good:** Challenging behaviour may have a sensory function. Some young people behave in a challenging way because, for them, it just feels good to do so at the time. This is especially relevant for those who feel an unrelenting sense of powerlessness as individuals within the systems that they exist in – in education and beyond.

4. **I want a reward:** Challenging behaviour may relate to the desire for a tangible reward. For example, a young child screaming in the back of a car may not want the attention of their parents. They may have learned that if they persistently scream, they will eventually get their favourite sweets to eat because their parents cannot bear the noise and need it to stop.

All schools should be clear about behaviour that is deemed to be challenging in their context and how they seek to find solutions. As well as offering support to students who are presenting with challenging behaviour, schools must also offer support to teachers who are searching for solutions to challenges. Teachers have needs too.

– Dr Tim O'Brien

Reality check

IDEA SNAPSHOT

In this final idea of the section, I raise some important issues about our education system. Teaching is a complex business and with the realities that all teachers face in classrooms up and down the land and across the world, sometimes a good lesson plan is not enough.

To date, I have been teaching for 23 years, which equates to roughly 950 lessons per year (give or take a few non-contact lessons here and there), which in turn equates to a possible grand total of 21,850 lessons taught! You, of course, will have your fair share of experience too and you will know, as well as I, that classrooms are complex environments. Our students literally have the world at their feet and all we can do as teachers is open doors for them. We will all be able to recall the numerous times we have imparted wisdom on our students, in the hope they heed our advice, grow up to respect each other and make a unique contribution to society.

In my time, I have taught up-and-coming footballers, Olympic athletes and popstars, but I have also taught a number of students who have grown up to be drug dealers and thieves, and (very sadly) intelligent young minds who have passed away from natural causes or prematurely in road accidents, house fires and other tragic incidents. When working with children, things will always go wrong, yet much of what we do in the classroom can alter their journey through life.

To achieve this, we must develop the confidence to deal with mistakes and external circumstances that are out of our control. These could be mistakes we make in our planning that then sprout up in a lesson or incidents that take place outside of school, which then culminate in a cataclysmic episode in class and make teaching and learning impossible. In many schools, the latter is a rare occurrence, but in more challenging settings, this could quite easily be a daily event. In his authentic book *The Confident Teacher*, teacher Alex Quigley neatly sums up the journey that every teacher must go on:

> 'We are constantly evolving our practice, adapting our moves and recognising the full game […] an expert teacher absorbs the complex past experiences.' (Quigley, 2016)

However, despite our best efforts to improve our practice and plan lessons that will have an impact on students, there are a variety of internal pressures that can stop even the best teacher in their tracks. These are often the result of pinch points in the academic year, which range from report writing season, illness and lack of curriculum time, to dealing with mixed-ability classes, being observed and heavy workloads. They all have a direct impact on the time available to create, modify and carry out lesson plans.

In some very extreme cases, lesson planning will be last on the agenda – with student safety being first. When I started teaching in Tottenham, North London, I considered a lesson to have been a success if a chair hadn't been flung across the room. Learning was right at the bottom of my to-do list. We have all had those lessons we dread and these situations, sadly, make teachers fearful. That's the reality. Teaching is complex and in some schools, I suspect, it is literally a battle zone.

Have we forgotten, then, that there is no one-size-fits-all method for teaching? That teaching is a lifelong journey with no perfect solution? Yet, our schools and our school systems place unwieldy demands on teachers to perform. In an increasingly high-stakes culture, we are destined to fail, especially if teachers are forced to use someone else's lesson plan template, to scribe lesson plans for every lesson, or submit plans a week in advance. You would be forgiven if you had forgotten that teachers are qualified professionals. Not everyone can keep a room full of thirty kids silent for an hour, or control an assembly and make every student in it feel empowered, or, with the mention of a verb of two, make every student fear for their life.

Confidence cannot be underestimated, but our system seeks to diminish what confidence our professionals have.

Wellbeing and mental health

At the time of writing, the 2016 School Workforce Census in England has just been published. In November 2015, this same census reported record numbers of teachers leaving the profession and teachers leaving more quickly than ever before.

In 2015, The Guardian reported that 'almost four out of ten teachers quit within a year of qualifying, with 11,000 leaving the profession before they have really begun their career' (Weale, 2015). In addition, evidence presented by the National Association of Schoolmasters Union of Women Teachers (NASUWT), which sampled 4,908 teachers across England, suggested 'one in ten teachers [takes] antidepressants to cope with work stresses' (NASUWT, 2016).

How is this acceptable? No wonder things are going wrong in the classroom if we are putting this much strain on our classroom teachers. The impact on teacher wellbeing is very concerning. Accountability is also certainly impacting on our students in terms of expectations and the pressures facing our young people. For teachers and students, the school environment is a pressure cooker that's been bubbling away for far too long.

At the time of writing, there is an ongoing and significant rise in mental health problems among young people. In the Queen's Speech on 21st June 2017, Her Majesty Queen Elizabeth II said:

> 'My government will reform mental health legislation and ensure that mental health is prioritised in the National Health Service in England.' (Cabinet Office and Prime Minister's Office, 10 Downing Street, 2017)

According to the mental health charity, YoungMinds, about 10% of young people aged 15-16 in England self-harm (YoungMinds, 2017). I can recall at least two students in each of the schools I have worked in as a senior teacher who have self-harmed in my presence. Once, I was covered in blood after pulling a student back as he repeatedly headbutted a wall. Another student showed me the razor blade he had just used to slash his abdomen. Thankfully, the number of students I have witnessed self-harming is small, but I know that many other students are affected by this too because there have been several cases that I have been informed about only as and when I have needed to know. Our schools and teachers are stretched, and we do not have the skills to be able to offer the support our young people need.

My childhood background with the social services, with having to deal with physical, sexual and drug abuse, death and self-harm have given me sufficient experience to be able to deal with these situations as an adult and as a teacher. Yet, I have never felt competent enough to offer expertise. Our job as teachers is first and foremost to teach. We know school is stressful and no matter how well we plan a lesson or tell a student how to behave, it sometimes just isn't enough. As a nation, we need a reality check. For most people working on the front line, not only in our schools, but also in our hospitals and our emergency services, who are battling to keep us safe from terrorism, every day is a struggle and the straw that breaks the camel's back is not a one-off event. We must invest in our national services.

If I think of the thousands of students in the schools I have worked in, most who have needed referrals to the Child and Adolescent Mental Health Services (CAMHS) are struggling with issues that manifest due to events outside of school, but support offered at home or in school is not sufficient. Occasionally, student behaviour displays itself in front of others as a cry for help. Teachers are not experts, nor are they expected to deal with mental illness. However, as a duty of care, every adult working with children must have the highest regard for safeguarding and, in whatever form, we must do what we can.

Sadly, recent changes to Educational Health Care (EHC) plans and requests have become a logistical nightmare. They are too time consuming and paperwork heavy. Getting one shot at building a case is virtually impossible for some schools and puts the needs of vulnerable students at a much higher risk.

Self–harm

Natasha Devon MBE is a writer and a social critic, who founded the Body Gossip education programme and Self-Esteem Team, designed to educate teenagers, teachers and parents about mental health and body image. On 30th August 2015, the DfE appointed Natasha as its first ever mental health champion for schools. One year later, her role was axed after she criticised the government's testing regime in schools. Below, Natasha offers an exclusive opinion on self-harm for readers of *Mark. Plan. Teach.*

'I've heard many people who have self-harmed speak about why it served a critical purpose for them, during a difficult period in their lives. For some, it provides a distraction from emotional pain. For others, it is a way of expressing difficult feelings physically, in a way others can understand. Many talk about self-harm in language traditionally associated with addiction, describing the rush they get in the immediate aftermath and the way they have to increase the severity of their behaviour over time in order to get the same 'high'. There's also a sub-set of young people who don't see self-harm as radically different from a piercing or a tattoo, using it to self-identify into a group they feel an affinity with.

Self-harm marks the intersection at which mental health, first aid and safeguarding become indistinguishable, making how teachers handle it crucial.

Whilst every case is different, my advice would be not to show disapproval or shock, but instead demonstrate a genuine desire to help, initially by providing physical first aid and then emotional support. Bear in mind that self-harm, like eating disorders, is shrouded in a bizarre pairing of secrecy and competitiveness, so you are likely to encounter a mixture of reticence and perverse pride. Try to replace the phrase 'attention seeking' with 'attention needing' in your mind.

Remember at all times that self-harm is in most cases a coping mechanism, so the ultimate aim is not to make the behaviour stop and nothing more. In fact, to do so might put the young person at increased risk of suicide since they no longer have an outlet for the difficult emotions they may be grappling with. By all means, suggest alternatives for distraction, self-expression and endorphin production, such as sport, creative writing, music, or even screaming or punching a pillow.

If you do recommend a student goes online for more information, make sure it's a forum that monitors its content, so they won't find themselves in a so-called 'pro-self-harm' environment (where techniques and triggering photos are shared between users). The Self-Harm Network is a good example of a safe website.

Finally, remember that no matter what your leadership team or parents might imply, it isn't your job to 'fix' the young person. You can be a sympathetic ear and a signpost towards further sources of support and information, but you are not a mental health professional and it is unreasonable to expect you to be.'

When I think about the challenges my colleagues face as they deal with the complexities of school life and the needs of the most vulnerable children in our society, I don't even know where to begin to put my thoughts in writing. I constantly wonder how it must be affecting their wellbeing.

Why do school leaders go around bullying staff, enforcing endless data consumption and detailed, written lesson planning on colleagues, pushing them further away from actually doing what's best for the children they teach? We work in complex environments and with some of the most challenging people in our society. We need to support one another and realise that teaching is more than just getting great examination results. Success is not just about going to university. For some children, just turning up to school is an achievement.

It is essential we don't lose sight of what is important.

Our future generations need good teachers. We need to demonstrate that teaching is more than a qualification. Our education system and our teachers should be given the autonomy to forget about teaching to the test and instead be able to nurture learning in our classrooms without the fear of external accountability, which is leading to increasing numbers of mental health issues in some of our most vulnerable children.

We must remember that sometimes, a great lesson plan is simply not sufficient and that's what makes teaching so vital and so rewarding.

Psychology and... teacher wellbeing

Ross highlights that there is no one-size-fits-all, perfect solution available for teaching. This may be one of the reasons why the teaching profession has been so susceptible to gimmicks and fads. In the search for a universal solution, one approach after another competes to become the only approach in town. Teachers do all that they can to make that approach work in their context. Then the approach falls into disrepute or fades into the mist. When this happens, the teaching profession cannot be seen to be in a state of not knowing – which is, by the way, a stimulating psychological state to be in – and the void must be filled. And so the process continues. Fortunately, becoming a more evidence-informed profession enables teachers to adopt an increasingly critical gaze and challenge taken-for-granted practices that, in the past, have been presented to them as indisputable common sense.

CONTINUES OVER PAGE

For decades, teachers have committed to government initiatives regularly imposed upon them without consultation. Then there is the accountability agenda. I recently conducted research for The Chartered College of Teaching, and it was evident that teachers in that research study had no problem at all with being accountable. Their concern was the way that accountability has been applied, creating a culture of fear. My view is that the current system of hyperaccountability places teachers in a state of manic vigilance that generates anxiety, guilt and stress.

All that I have described so far inevitably impacts upon teacher wellbeing. The situation has to change. The wellbeing needs of teachers have been overlooked for too long. However, identifying teacher wellbeing needs is not straightforward because wellbeing itself is a contested construct. Wellbeing can be understood from many perspectives, including mental health, physical, psychological and spiritual. Wellbeing can be seen as having dimensions that are measurable, yet it can also be seen as culturally constructed and therefore shifting in meaning and interpretations. We also have to consider whether teacher wellbeing actually exists as a separate domain of wellbeing and, if so, whether it is qualitatively different to wellbeing in any other profession and why.

I propose that one way of understanding wellbeing is to think about unwellbeing; what would be missing that would have a negative impact on wellbeing. What would that be for you? Perhaps professional autonomy? Enjoyment? Being valued for what you do? Collaboration? Or a sense of meaning and purpose?

– Dr Tim O'Brien

Section 2: Summary

Planning is deliberately positioned right in the middle of the **Mark. Plan. Teach.** cycle because I believe it is the pinnacle of everything a good teacher must be able to do. Providing feedback to your students through assessment and marking (while ensuring that verbal feedback becomes part of your classroom routine) will enable you to check your students' understanding of their work. If you do this regularly, assessment and marking will inform all aspects of your short-, medium- and long-term planning. It will allow you to adapt your lessons (either by careful design or on the spot) to the needs of your students and help them become more engaged in their learning. As you interact with students, you will be able to see their progress (or lack of) and this will inform future teaching and possibly even help shape future schemes of work, differentiation needs and opportunities for intervention.

No matter how you look at it, planning is a pillar in the **Mark. Plan. Teach.** cycle and it supports marking, feedback and teaching.

As a reminder, here are the headlines of this section of the book: ten ideas to help your lesson planning inform your marking and teaching and ultimately enable you to have a greater impact on your students' learning:

1. Be clear and precise about the knowledge and skills you want students to *learn*, not what you want them to do. It is important to shift the focus away from activities to what we are *learning* and why. Only then will the teaching and learning have any substance and you can ensure that students will have a chance of learning and making progress.

2. Apply the 'why?' test to all learning activities, including homework, so your planning is designed to facilitate learning and not to keep students busy. Make sure you can explain to students clearly and succinctly why they are learning things to deepen understanding and increase engagement.

3. Integrate imaginative teaching strategies, such as storytelling, into your lessons to keep your students engaged but plan how and when to use them carefully to ensure they impact on learning.

4. Embed stickability into your lesson planning. Think about what learning should stick in the minds of your students and the key points you want your students to remember and bring back to the next lesson. Teach students study strategies that involve practice retrieval and spaced practice to help them make their learning stick.

5. Plan to keep students in the struggle zone to ensure they feel sufficiently challenged but not stressed or anxious. Embed assessment methods, such as questioning, into your lesson plans to help you achieve this.

6. In lessons that get off to a flying start, students learn more purposefully from the beginning. Simple flying starts – that don't require hours of planning – often have the greatest impact and are the perfect opportunity to embed literacy into lesson plans.

7. Differentiation should be planned over time to ensure a quality first teaching approach that meets the needs of all students. Use seating plans based on your knowledge of each student to support this. Planning should also maximise the use of any additional adults in the room.

8. Stockpile resources and strategies that you can pull out of a hat next time a lesson doesn't quite go to plan or you need to fill five minutes at the end of class. With just a little forward planning, you can create a bank of ideas that will help you out of a tricky situation, while still impacting on learning.

9. Be aware that when dealing with challenging behaviour, you may need to change your lesson plan on the spot. Knowing your individual students, their specific contexts and motivations for an outburst in class will help you provide the right intervention at the right time, and it is important that your school grants you the flexibility to do this.

10. Finally, when it comes to lesson planning, we all need a reality check once in a while, especially those involved in decisions about our national education system. External accountability is impacting the mental health and wellbeing of our teachers and our students. Teaching is about more than examination results and just sometimes, a great lesson plan is simply not enough.

Section 3:
TEACH.

There is no such thing as a quintessential teaching style, and those who have mentored us – or at least those who mentored us *well* – will want every teacher to find out what works best for them and their students, rather than adopt a specific style or approach.

We've all encountered good teachers and bad teachers in our own school experiences, and we all have ideas about what makes one teacher better than another, but all teachers will, of course, teach differently in different settings. If you are reading this book as a teacher – and there is a high chance that you are – then I know I am preaching to the converted. You will be able to think of some amazing teachers you have worked with and be able to jot down on paper what it is that makes them so great.

I wonder if there is room among all the good teachers in our schools, colleges and universities for a maverick teacher. I used to think so, but over the past few years, I've started to believe that individualism is not tolerated in some schools.

Admittedly, a maverick can be a risk. Eric Cantona – a Manchester United footballer in the 1990s – is a classic example of this. He was football heaven and hell. A talented player, famous for being larger than life, physically strong, hard working and a tenacious forward, he combined technical skill with creativity, power and goal scoring ability. Despite his incredible footwork and vision, however, his notoriety came from an off-the-ball incident many thought far outweighed the greater good he brought to the team and was in fact detrimental to his (and the team's) overall success.

However we choose to define a maverick teacher, whether risk taking, creative or unorthodox, I am certain we can all remember someone in our school who has broken the mould. I am confident that some readers may also consider themselves to be somewhat maverick.

As for myself, I was promoted in my third year of teaching. I was 26 and had barely mastered the classroom. In my heyday as a middle leader, some six or seven years later, I was at my most creative and would have considered myself to be a maverick. I was confident, experimental and had overcome the difficulties we all face in our first year of teaching, but I was also a world apart from the policies of senior leadership. Despite leading a team of 13 staff and being on the cusp of school leadership myself, I was still a huge step away from having any whole-school perspective. I rarely observed colleagues outside my own department in a climate where all schools were grading lessons but colleagues were only observed three hours per academic year. This was 15 years ago but it is still happening in many schools today.

Back then, it was rare to observe another teacher unless it was your job or you had been told to do so. It was often voluntary and something you did in the little free or non-contact time you had available. Whole-school systems for using observations to develop and help coach colleagues (Section 3, Idea 10, p. 160) were few and far between. I had also not yet been faced with having to support or challenge experienced teachers who were reliable and all-round solid but whose personal confidence sometimes undermined the collective school vision because they would ignore policies and procedures. I had not yet understood, or been encouraged to recognise, that these behaviours may not be helpful to the overall success of a school. I was still developing a repertoire for observing a wide range of teaching practice.

Now, 15 years on, my experience of lesson observations has grown significantly. If I were to take a guess, I would say I have observed thousands of lessons taught by the 500-plus teachers I have had the pleasure of working with. I have been in a position in three schools where I have had the responsibility of observing 100 teachers in each setting. I recognise that as a senior teacher, I was not teaching as much as I would have liked to and I lost my maverick edge. I had fewer opportunities to take risks, be creative and interpret school policies in order to be in a position where I could teach with confidence and encourage students to love learning. But, I was placed in a privileged position where I could observe, support and challenge colleagues who might well have been undermining each other – never because they took risks or used a particular teaching style but because they ignored procedures or (more likely) were inundated with requests to 'do this', 'fill this in', 'complete that', 'go there at this time' and so forth.

With this vast array of experience in lesson observations, I can say with confidence that one size does *not* fit all. The Grim Reaper is clear, and school leaders should be too, that we must not champion one particular style of teaching over another.

So, with all this in mind, let's go back to my opening paragraphs about what you think makes a good or bad teacher. Make a note of a few characteristics that spring to mind:

Good qualities	Bad qualities

Now, take a look at your list above. Who did you have in mind when you wrote the list of good qualities? What makes them special? How long have they been teaching? Are they a maverick? Do you find yourself learning from them to this day? Does this person still have a learning mindset? What makes them vary wildly to the person (or set of characteristics) you have described on the right? Which teacher is most likely to follow your school's policies and procedures?

Teaching in line with school policy

Teaching in line with school policy, beyond my formative (and occasionally painful) years as a newly qualified teacher, was a steep learning curve when I became a middle leader. Mastering the art of teaching, as well as learning the trade of middle leadership, was a tough journey. However, as my confidence in experimenting with teaching evolved, my willingness to take risks and my subject confidence both soared. Middle leadership was the happiest time of my teaching career. Growing into the role of middle leader exposed me to a wider world beyond the classroom. I soon realised the need for every teacher, including myself and my colleagues in other departments, to be working in line with school policy.

This would ensure that colleagues did not undermine each other and, more importantly, students would know that there would be no slippage, no gaps in the system that would be exposed between classrooms. We could be confident that what one colleague was saying or doing in one classroom would be more or less the same as what another was saying or doing in the classroom next door or even on the other side of the school building. How often have your students quoted the school rules back to you? If this happens regularly, the students clearly understand the rules and they must be working! Understanding the bigger picture and collective purpose of the school, and therefore why teaching in line with school policy is so important, is something that is difficult to communicate to classroom teachers who don't have the opportunity to observe each other. I, for one, only grasped the importance of school policy when I observed colleagues as a young middle leader.

I believe that a good teacher is one who is given the freedom to teach in a way that suits them and their students. A good teacher takes risks, is creative, enjoys their subject and develops their students' love of learning, but also understands the importance of remaining within a defined set of boundaries and expectations for the greater good of the school.

How can we genuinely improve teaching and learning?

In this section, I offer a range of teaching ideas that will help you to put Sections 1 and 2 into practice. With clear explanations, teachers can make learning stick (Section 3, Idea 1, p. 119 and Idea 2, p. 124), and with an established culture, high expectations, routines and conditions, teachers can go with the flow of learning, confidently adapting their lessons to meet the needs of students (Section 3, Idea 3, p. 128), all the while using questioning to check learning has stuck (Section 3, Idea 5, p. 137).

Encouraging teachers to take risks and 'go with the flow' in classrooms is all fine and dandy, but teachers need a safe and rewarding climate in which they feel comfortable to do this. We know that this is rare in our current school system, but as David Weston says, 'if we want the best for our children... [we need to] do the best for our teachers' (Weston, 2015). This section will, therefore, also look at what school leaders can do to introduce and embed a simple teaching and learning policy that enables teachers to teach without fear of tick-box templates, stringent lesson plans or choking schemes of work (Section 3, Idea 4, p. 131). It will also consider how a culture of continued professional development (CPD) can be built into a setting by using lesson observation to develop teachers, not judge them. Staff should be given time to observe each other's lessons, to learn from one another and to reflect on their own practice (Section 3, Idea 8, p. 153). A system of coaching can also work wonders to encourage staff to take control of their own CPD, develop their practice and, ultimately, believe in what they are doing on a daily basis to improve the lives of the students they teach.

Direct instruction

IDEA SNAPSHOT

In Section 2, Idea 2, p. 67, I discussed the importance of students understanding *why* they are learning what they are learning and I explored how you can embed this into your lesson planning to deepen understanding and increase engagement. When you are teaching, it's essential that you are explicit about the learning outcomes and the keywords that form the foundations of your lesson; students must understand the knowledge and skills you want them to learn and the language they are expected to understand and apply. This idea looks at how this can be achieved through a combination of direct instruction and 'nudge theory'.

The standard method of sharing learning outcomes and keywords is by writing them on the board at the start of the lesson, asking students to copy them down and referring to them when appropriate throughout the lesson and particularly at the end of the lesson. However, we know (and have seen in Section 2, Idea 2, p. 67) that this is guff! In most cases, particularly if you are new to teaching, you should share learning outcomes and keywords (and you have probably been told to do so), but students should not copy them down. This is a 'control' activity, not a learning activity, and you should stop doing it, unless you have a really difficult class and you need, on the rare occasion, to apply a control strategy in order to calm students down and assist them on their learning journey. After all, good behaviour is a precursor for learning in any setting and without it, all teachers will struggle.

Nevertheless, copying down the learning outcomes is definitely not a flying start to learning (see Section 2, Idea 6, p. 86) and should be used as a last ditch attempt to focus the class, not as a routine to open every lesson.

There are much more sophisticated variations of sharing and helping students to understand the learning outcomes available. We saw one in Section 2, Idea 2: Marcella McCarthy's 'Invisible Sun', where the teacher keeps the outcomes hidden from view and asks students to unpick what the learning objectives are as they move through the lesson.

Here are some further variations that you might like to try in your teaching:

- Ask students to remind you of the learning outcomes and keywords from the previous lesson and give them time to speculate on what they might be for this lesson.

- Complete the first activity you have planned (it could be a flying start) and then ask the class what they think the learning outcomes and keywords might be.

- Teach the entire lesson and then ask students what they think the learning outcomes and keywords might have been.

When it comes to keywords, it is essential to embed them into the lesson and into the language you use with your students. Keywords mentioned at the beginning of class and then never again serve no purpose. If your high expectations are represented in your language, at least some of the keywords you are using will not be commonly understood by the class and the process of explaining them (and enabling students to use them) will be a very significant part of your lesson. By definition, the number of keywords you introduce should be small – no more than two or three per lesson. It is a high-level teaching skill to be able to build your lesson around a couple of keywords, so see Section 2, Idea 6, p. 86 for some more guidance.

Direct instruction and 'nudge theory'

Professor John Hattie says that 'teacher clarity' has a positive influence on student achievement. Hattie defines 'teacher clarity' as 'organization, explanation, examples and guided practice [...] of student learning' and he believes that 'clarity of speech [is] a prerequisite of teacher clarity' (Hattie, 2009). I see 'teacher clarity' as the importance of clearly communicating the intentions of a lesson and the success criteria, namely the learning outcomes and keywords and, in fact, clearly communicating all direct instruction or teacher-led learning. Whenever your lesson involves direct teaching, you should ensure all instructions are delivered clearly so students know what they are doing at any given point in the lesson. The MINT strategy is one way of doing this successfully.

The MINT strategy

For a long time, I have applied the MINT strategy to everything I do in the classroom, and I also now use it in teacher training sessions and other aspects of life outside school. It's a perfect example of how to use 'teacher clarity' in the direct instruction elements of your lesson because it helps you ensure that all instructions are delivered with clarity and in bite-sized chunks. Let's look at how it works.

Firstly, the acronym MINT stands for:

M = Materials

I = In or out of seats

N = Noise level

T = Time

To explain further, here's how I would go about using MINT when teaching a lesson:

Materials: simply means resources to be used; do not overcomplicate things – if there are five objects in a box, state the box and not the five individual objects.

In or out of seats: even in a practical subject, not every lesson will involve activities out of seats and in more theoretical subjects, such as maths, students may need to work around the classroom, solving problems with peers.

Noise level*: be clear about the accepted volume.

- Volume 1 = No talking; individual, silent work
- Volume 2 = Paired discussions
- Volume 3 = Whole-class discussion

Time: specify clearly the time needed to complete the activity, including final warning.

*As much as I detest noise-o-meters when used to monitor whether classroom noise levels are acceptable or not, they can work wonders in primary settings and with 11 to 14 year olds to help students learn how to manage their own classroom discussions.

Here's an example showing exactly how I might apply the MINT strategy in any part of a lesson, using it as a framework for direct instruction:

M: 'You will need a piece of A3 paper, a pencil, a ruler and this pink A5 worksheet.'

I: 'You will be working out of your seat, moving slowly around the classroom, visiting various sources on display.'

N: 'The noise I would like you to maintain is a quiet conversation in your groups.'

T: 'The time you have to do this is seven minutes. I will also give you a final one minute warning before we stop.'

Unconditional positive regard and 'nudge theory'

Relating to 'teacher clarity' and direct instruction, 'unconditional positive regard' (UPR) is a concept first brought to my attention by Hywel Roberts in his book *Oops! Helping Children Learn Accidentally* (Roberts, 2012). The term was first devised by the psychologist Carl Rogers and it describes how children should be accepted and supported, irrespective of their actions. Even the most challenging and humble of students need UPR offered through 'teacher clarity' and direct instruction. Those not exposed to UPR may come to see themselves in negative ways. Clear and direct UPR helps children accept responsibility for themselves, aids their personal growth and allows them to be spontaneous without fearing that others might lose respect for them.

However, 'nudge theory' argues that using positive reinforcement or indirect suggestion is far more effective than direct instruction or enforcement when trying to persuade people to do something. As first proposed by Richard Thaler and Cass Sunstein in their book *Nudge*, 'nudge theory' suggests that spending lots of time *telling* students to do something or making rules is not very effective and becomes even less effective over time (Thaler and Sunstein, 2009).

There are lots of examples of good behaviour management where 'nudge theory' is used. Rather than reprimanding children, for example, we may praise other children near them for doing the right thing. I have used this in countless behaviour scenarios to deflect positive behaviours onto nearby students who are either misbehaving or are disrupting the teaching and learning. It takes practice, but it does work.

Other examples of 'nudge theory' include arranging the chairs and tables in our classrooms to facilitate certain behaviours that we require in that lesson. Teachers can also reward students for doing the right thing, such as arriving in the classroom with their ties done up or having their planners out on their desks to start the lesson. Teachers then allocate rewards throughout the lesson, referencing 'correct' behaviours identified earlier, to embed actions they want to see in their students.

In my opinion, both direct instruction and 'nudge theory' have a place in every classroom, so teachers offer students clarity but do not constantly *tell* them to do things or make rules. You should share learning objectives and keywords in your lessons but this could be done through direct instruction and 'teacher clarity' one week, then the next you could 'nudge' students to decode the objectives and keywords independently. Combining these two techniques will help deepen your students' understanding of what you want them to learn in your lessons and why.

EVIDENCE

Direct instruction is by no means the only effective approach to teaching, but it does work better than many other teaching techniques. Direct instruction is teacher centred but it does not require teachers to entertain their students and it is not the same as rote learning; like most other teaching approaches, it asks students to be persistent and reap the rewards of hard work.

Research from the Education Development Trust and the University of Oxford (Ko et al., 2014) demonstrates the value of direct instruction. In a review of the literature, the research found a number of studies provided evidence that teacher-directed approaches have a strong positive effect on attainment, especially among younger students and those from a more disadvantaged background. The research goes on to claim that although direct instruction is important in group and paired work:

> 'organising students as a whole class for a significant proportion of a lesson helps to maximise their contact with the teacher so every student benefits from the teaching and interaction for sustained periods of time.'

This suggests that direct instruction might be the most efficient way of teaching large classes of students effectively.

Most importantly, however, the report found evidence that 'learning can be greatly accelerated if instructional presentations are clear, minimise misinterpretations and facilitate generalisations'. This just shows how essential 'teacher clarity' is in all elements of direct instruction and is backed up by John Hattie's 'ranking of effect sizes'. According to Hattie, direct instruction has an impact of $d=0.60$ on student learning and achievement, while 'teacher clarity' has an even greater impact of $d-0.75$ (Hattie, 2009).

I have witnessed some superb direct teaching in my career, notably the work of former colleagues, James and Dianne Murphy of Thinking Reading Ltd. They have developed an intensive one-to-one, evidence-based intervention for struggling readers. Students experience rapid, lasting success, typically progressing one year for every three hours of the intervention. A case study on the Thinking Reading website puts this in context:

> 'Student B was found to be reading six years behind her chronological age when assessed. She gained six and a half years over the eleven months of her programme.' (Thinking Reading Ltd, 2017)

It's clear that direct instruction, when conducted with 'teacher clarity', can have a significant impact on progress and achievement, but it would be interesting to understand *why* direct instruction works. I personally suspect that a confident, consistent teacher, secure with subject knowledge and clear expectations of behaviour for learning in the classroom, may be the answer.

Modelling

IDEA SNAPSHOT

Modelling is an important method of direct instruction (see Section 3, Idea 1, p. 119). There are a number of modelling strategies that can be applied to help students develop key skills in literacy and numeracy in all settings and subject areas. This idea will explore some of the best.

We are all teachers of literacy and numeracy, regardless of the age group and the subject we teach. The quality of a student's written and oral language, namely whether it contains sharp, accurate and well-developed descriptions, explanations and vocabulary, is a significant determinant of progress. A strong mathematical grounding is also beneficial in a wide variety of subjects, including the STEM subjects (science, technology, engineering and maths), but also geography, computing, art, PE, economics and so on.

When it comes to teaching literacy and numeracy, modelling strategies are essential. By explaining or demonstrating to students exactly what is expected of them (while also keeping expectations high), students will be able to respond more effectively to the tasks you set them. Let's take a look at some modelling strategies that you could implement quickly and easily in your classroom to have an impact on your students' literacy and numeracy skills.

Reading

When tackling longer or more challenging texts, **reciprocal teaching** will enable students to support one another to fully digest what they are reading. Reciprocal teaching is an instructional activity in which students become the teacher in small group reading sessions, equipped with a straightforward set of reading comprehension strategies:

1. Summarising – highlighting the key ideas in the text.

2. Questioning – asking questions about the text (such as whether anything is unclear or puzzling and how the text relates to previous learning).

3. Clarifying – addressing confusing parts of the text and attempting to answer the questions posed in Stage 2.

4. Predicting – thinking about what might happen later in the story or what the author might say in the next section of the text.

Teachers model to students how to guide group discussions using these four strategies. Students are then split into groups and guide their own discussions about the text. One student could lead the entire discussion or the students could divide the four techniques between them and lead on each in turn. The teacher provides assistance as and when necessary.

Writing

Oral rehearsal in preparation for an upcoming writing task is essential. Particularly for students with English as an additional language, the opportunity to rehearse writing by discussing ideas with a partner or in small groups in standard English not only improves content but also helps develop literacy.

There are a number of strategies you could use here, including group discussions and presentations, but one approach that is especially effective is **think-pair-share**. In this technique, students first work independently, *thinking* about how they might approach the task, what they might like to write about and how they could put their ideas into words. The students then *pair* up to discuss their ideas and develop them further. Finally, the teacher facilitates a whole-class discussion, asking the pairs to *share* what they have come up with. This builds a model of how the students might approach the writing task and gives them the confidence to put their ideas down on paper.

Another simple, yet sophisticated, classroom technique that can build writing skills in all settings is **I do, we do, you do**. This is an important strategy that can be used whenever you expect students to complete any form of extended writing. **I do, we do, you do** is a form of scaffolding that involves:

- Direct instruction: the teacher models the learning activity.

- Guided instruction: the teacher and student complete the learning activity simultaneously; the teacher continues to model but also checks what the students are doing and provides prompts where necessary.

- Independent practice: the student completes the learning activity alone (or in pairs or small groups) without guidance from the teacher; the teacher can provide feedback on the students' work once complete.

Numeracy

Students often don't appreciate the value of numeracy but as teachers, it is our job to help them understand just how important it is. Numeracy includes not only significant aspects of what is taught in mathematics, but also the ability to use numbers and solve problems in real life and across the curriculum.

In fact, numeracy is relevant to all subjects and includes:

- Reasoning
- Problem solving
- Decision making
- Shapes
- Use of space
- Measures
- Calculations
- Data handling…
- …as well as anything taught within the mathematics curriculum.

When you are teaching anything that is numeracy related, you should **make it explicit** that you are doing so. You could use a **visualiser** or your **interactive whiteboard** to model a problem relating to your lesson content and show mathematical working, so students can visually relate the problem to concepts they may have learnt in maths lessons. This will help students see the relationships between subjects and instil in them the importance of maths across the curriculum and in everyday life.

The process of modelling an activity, then asking students to complete it independently or in small groups will enable students to put their learning into practice, helping them to retain information learnt and skills gained. Practical application will also help students to appreciate the value of the information and skills they are learning, not only in the subject being taught but also across the curriculum and in real-life situations, enhancing their engagement and therefore impacting on progress. As always, memory (and forgetting – see Section 1, Idea 6, p. 34) has a significant role to play in learning, be it subject-specific or cross-curricular content. Read on to find out more about memory from Dr Tim O'Brien…

Psychology and...
memory

Memory is complex and multifaceted: autobiographical memory, episodic memory, semantic memory, short-term memory, long-term memory, declarative memory, non-declarative memory, context-dependent memory…

Let's start with autobiographical memory and move on to memory and its association with learning. When we describe incidents that have happened to us years ago, we often say, 'I remember as if it were yesterday'. The problem is, we don't. We like to think that our memory consists of events and experiences that we recollect and reliably reproduce. The problem is, it doesn't. Your memory is not an infallible archive of your life experiences. Remembering is a process that involves different parts of your brain communicating with each other. When you remember something, your memory is prone to errors. Memory is malleable and changeable and our memories can be notoriously unreliable. They can be so unreliable that they can even be false. We construct and reconstruct what we think happened to us in the past rather than retrieve and recall exactly what did happen. The proposition here is that your memory is a series of narratives.

Learning requires memory; remembering and forgetting are components of learning. Earlier in this book, when talking about making and embracing mistakes, I referred to a specific cognitive four-stage model of learning processes (p. 33). Cognitive models often raise interesting issues about learning and memory, especially short-term and long-term memory. They help us to remain conscious that short-term memory is inevitably susceptible to cognitive overload and remind us that overload will have a negative impact on a person's learning capability. In relation to long-term memory, cognitive models remind us that what we have learned can become increasingly unrequired and may appear to be ultimately redundant and hence forgotten. However, what had previously been learned can be brought from unconscious to conscious awareness through the process of cognition – by thinking about what has been forgotten. In relation to the process of learning, long-term memory is central to making the unfamiliar become familiar again; offering a range of memory cues can help this happen.

Conceptualising memory as being malleable reminds teachers and students to accept not only that forgetting is part of learning but also that forgetting can enable learning. It encourages teachers to plan optimistic teaching and learning interactions to allow students to engage in the cognitive (and emotional) rigour involved in making meaning so that they increase their potential to retain and remember what they have learned over time.

– Dr Tim O'Brien

IDEA 3

The flow

IDEA SNAPSHOT

Every teacher should have the confidence to 'go with the learning' when they teach a lesson. This means ensuring flow in the delivery of teaching content to enable greater progress. This freedom is far more important than following a lesson plan but it must be encouraged and supported by a whole-school culture that rejects checklists and gradings, and allows teachers to make mistakes and learn from them. Just think about what happens when a flowing stream meets a large rock or a dam. It eventually works out a new path and moves on. This is exactly what you should be doing in your lessons.

T eachers are fearful of taking risks in schools where a growing climate of accountability is endemic, but often, allowing teachers to take risks and learn from mistakes is the best way of improving teaching and learning in our schools.

John Hattie ranked 'collective teacher efficacy' the second most influential factor on student achievement in 2015, meaning that if any classroom strategy is to be effective, it must be underpinned by good teaching across the board. If schools wish to roll out a one-size-fits-all approach to teaching and learning, then it will only ever be as good as every teacher in every classroom. Good teaching will thrive only if there is a culture in the school that is devoid of checklists, evaluations and gradings and allows every teacher to make mistakes and learn from them.

But is this achievable or is this an impossible ask? Can teachers really allow lessons to be loose and should they take risks? Well, I've only ever worked in challenging schools where the pressure is so immense that a one-size-fits-all approach appears to be the best solution. However, I know that if schools and classrooms are to be successful, we must allow teachers and students to go with the flow.

For me, going with the flow means 'going with the learning' to enable greater progress. 'Going with the learning' allows teachers to deviate from their lesson plans as and when necessary to ensure learning is taking place. It is about valuing teachers who intuitively recognise whether students have learnt what they have been taught and who can adjust the lesson accordingly. This freedom is far more important than following an overly detailed lesson plan, enforcing a tick box culture or pleasing an imaginary (or even real) inspector. Lesson planning does still need to be thorough, however, otherwise there is nothing for teachers to deviate from. 'Winging it' might be possible in experienced hands, but it is not desirable and definitely not professional.

Here are my top tips for 'going with the flow':

- Before you can 'go with the learning', you must first be clear about the knowledge and skills you want students to learn and take away from the lesson. In your lesson planning, make sure you shift your focus away from the activities you want students to complete and instead think about what you want students to learn and why. For more on this, see Section 2, Idea 1, p. 61.

- Ensure you have a secure overview of the starting points, progress and context of every student you are teaching (see Section 1, Idea 1, p. 6). This will help you adapt your lesson plans on the spot to meet the specific needs of the students in your class.

- When students are completing a task, keep moving around and sit at each student's desk in turn, working with them closely. Listen, rather than talk. That way, you will be able to spot the students who are progressing and those who may need a helping hand, so you can decide where your lesson needs to go next to maximise learning.

- Mark work 'live' in lesson time, with the students by your side, so you can see immediately how your students are progressing and which specific areas they need to improve (see Section 1, Idea 3, p. 17). You will then know whether you can move on to the next phase of learning or whether there are any particular aspects you need to re-teach.

- Use questioning regularly in your lessons to check whether learning has stuck and if not, adjust your lesson plan accordingly (see Section 3, Idea 5, p. 137).

- Stockpile resources and activities that you can pull out of a hat to help you recap on and reinforce the key learning if you sense that something just hasn't stuck (see Section 2, Idea 8, p. 97).

Many lessons do not work out the way they were intended. Sometimes, knowledge and skills do not stick and need to be re-taught. An unexpected disruption might mean that activities need to be shortened or lengthened or done in a different order. Don't feel restricted by your lesson plan! The point of a lesson is to maximise learning, not deliver a plan. It is more important that your students grasp the key learning, rather than complete all the activities you had planned for the lesson, and the only way to do this is to 'go with the learning' and ensure flow in your delivery of teaching content.

Psychology and... flow

Ross refers to a concept of 'flow' occurring in various teaching contexts. Flow is also a well-researched psychological concept. One psychologist in particular, Mihaly Csikszentmihalyi, is well known for conceptualising and researching the psychological architecture of flow.

Csikszentmihalyi (2008) describes flow in terms of it being a state of consciousness where attention becomes a form of energy that promotes a merging of action and awareness, and produces deep levels of enjoyment. Being in a psychological state of flow involves an awareness of, and immersion in, the integrated harmony of what we are experiencing. Not only can a person lose track of time when in flow, they can also lose track of self. Flow creates an experience where there is a complete absence of worry about our own inadequacies because we are concentrated fully on the activity that we are engaged in. When we experience flow, there is no room left for our attention to be distracted towards self-scrutiny as that shifts attention and will naturally break the flow state. Attention is seen as the essential tool for optimising our experience and thus creating flow.

Csikszentmihalyi's research proposes that there are specific external conditions that promote the achievement of flow. Flow can occur when we feel challenged by an activity but are consciously aware that our skills are well matched to the challenges that the activity involves. You will have observed that if skills are not well matched to an activity, the level of challenge will generate anxiety and stress. If an activity is not well matched to skills, lack of challenge will generate boredom and disengagement.

My intention here has been to describe flow in a way that might allow you to connect it to your teaching context in a practical manner. I would also like to raise some broad questions about flow that teachers interested in reflection and action research might want to explore further. Questions like:

- Is it possible to create flow in educational settings?

- Is it easier to intentionally create flow in subjects such as music and PE than it is in subjects such as physics and Spanish?

- Is the experience of flow qualitatively different in early years, primary, secondary and specialist provision?

- Does pedagogic orientation influence the conditions and experience of flow?

- Can a teacher's understanding of flow help to remove barriers to learning for students who experience social, emotional and mental health difficulties?

– Dr Tim O'Brien

What every teacher should do...

IDEA SNAPSHOT

Make sure your students are working harder than you, not necessarily in every lesson but *over time*. Remember, though, that teaching in your classroom will only ever be as effective as the teaching taking place in the room next door to you. If you are in

a leadership position within your school, it is therefore important to embed a simple, evidence-based teaching and learning policy that can reduce teacher workload and maximise student progress. If you're not yet in a leadership position, discuss this idea with your managers. It might just lead to a better way of working for you, your colleagues and your students.

n Jim Smith's fantastic book, *The Lazy Teacher's Handbook*, he suggests that all students must be working harder than the teacher (Smith, 2010). Most teachers and observers would agree. This is by far the preferred stance in all classrooms: the teacher leads and facilitates the learning and students contribute, working on their own, in pairs or in groups and making progress. Lots of it! But how can we ensure students are working harder than teachers?

Firstly, I would argue that 'working harder' means working harder *over time*, rather than in a one-off lesson. The latter is particularly difficult to evidence when being observed and is almost certainly a myth generated by those attending conferences and then interpreting frameworks in their own place of work. Having the students work harder than the teacher is a level of classroom pace that certainly cannot be sustained in every lesson even by the best of us. How teachers perform on a cold Monday morning will be very different from how they teach on a sweltering Friday afternoon. You should never be asked to demonstrate 'students working hard' in a single lesson with, for example, students doing jazzy hands-on activities to entertain a classroom guest and give the impression of a busy, fun and lively classroom. Is this 'hard work' or is it 'looking busy'? And critically, what is the learning and what progress is being made?

If a variety of sources are consulted, evidence of students 'working hard' over a sustained period of time should speak for itself. The most obvious things to look out for are evidence of learning and progress in students' work and the teacher's secure overview of student data, including starting points and current attainment (see Section 1, Idea 1, p. 6). Other sources of evidence might include student conversations, routines, classroom expectations, displays, presentation of work, relationships in the classroom and teacher command, to name but a few.

Ultimately, it is the students who have to perform in the examination, the controlled assessment, the job interview and in their working lives. Your students must have the expectation that when they come to your lessons, they will think and work hard for sustained periods. This does not mean that whole-class teaching is discouraged, or that you are always expected to be a facilitator, but over time, the students must work harder than you.

Your planning is, of course, key to this, particularly the structure of the lesson and how you adapt longer activities when teaching. The start of the lesson can set the tone. You could encourage your students to come in and immediately start working unprompted while you meet and greet (see Section 2, Idea 6, p. 86). If you are new to teaching or you have a new class, you may well feel for some time as though you are the person working the hardest by far. It should be your ambition to reverse that. This is an essential element of student self-regulation. Do not pander to it; challenge it. Teach the learning behaviours you want to see and stick with them.

However, it is also important to consider how we can adopt and embed research-based strategies across an entire setting to enable students to make progress and encourage them to work harder than the teacher in all their classes. Remember, we know from John Hattie that with 'collective teacher efficacy' across an organisation, overall student progress will be greater (see Section 3, Idea 3, p. 128). So, what do we want our teachers to be able to do to help students make progress? What would you want to see teachers doing consistently in your school to make every teacher's job easier and to impact on learning?

The term 'common vernacular' was a poignant phrase I heard used by principal Alex Thomas (Capital City Academy, London), when I visited his school just as I was starting to research a coaching methodology and dialogue to replace formal lesson observations in my school (see Section 3, Idea 10, p. 160). In many ways, this visit formed the beginnings of a common framework that was adapted into a teaching and learning policy that I co-wrote with my headteacher.

Thomas' common vernacular – or at least the phrase – prompted my research into what common traits could be found in effective teachers and what research-based strategies they use. I wondered how these research-based strategies could be adopted in a script for questioning and for conversations between teachers when they were coaching each other. I also wondered how this could be simplified into a series of coaching prompts, that is to say a common vernacular for teachers to use when developing other teachers in short, focused lesson observations.

Developing this common vernacular then evolved into a short policy that formed the basis of a *Mark. Plan. Teach.* framework that would be used to develop consistency across the entire school. Unbeknownst to me, this would later become the foundations of this book! (See more about that in the Introduction, p. xvi.) We had weekly conversations about this framework and we tinkered with it and debated ideas every month with all staff. Finally, a one-page summary was written and used to communicate expectations and maintain consistency in each and every classroom.

This was delivered in three ways:

- A one-page summary explaining what we would expect from all teachers, in terms of marking, planning and teaching.

- Behind the one-page summary were explicit details, definitions, examples and exemplar material.

- Training, consultation and discussion sessions with all staff.

Depending on how much you've read of this book, you probably already have a sense of what this teaching and learning policy might entail but here it is, simplified into three sentences below. It is what I now call 'the simplest teaching and learning policy in the world'!

The simplest teaching and learning policy in the world!

- **Mark:** feedback that is regular and diagnostic, so that teachers have a secure overview of where students are going.

- **Plan:** lesson plans that are clear and consider 'why' students are learning, so that a quality first approach can meet the needs of all students.

- **Teach:** instructions delivered thoughtfully with explicit use of language, so that students understand what's being asked of them, engage with the lesson and then act on feedback.

There are many different teaching strategies that could be implemented to achieve the above and you will find several that I have used throughout my career in this book. They can, of course, work in isolation but what if I could come up with a shortlist of strategies that could be used by all teachers across my school to really make an impact on student progress? And what if I made using these strategies a minimum requirement for all teachers?

With this in mind, here is my shortlist. They are strategies that I know work for me, my students and the school context in which I am working. The list is deliberately concise and workable so that all teachers can deploy them successfully as and when they are required. Unless all teachers understand them and use them effectively, then they are as useful as a teacher who has been up all night before a school inspection – useless!

So here you go:

- The yellow box (see Section 1, Idea 3, p. 17)
- Think-pair-share (see Section 3, Idea 2, p. 124)
- I do, we do, you do (see Section 3, Idea 2, p. 124)
- Pose, pause, pounce, bounce (see Section 3, Idea 5, p. 137)

Now, over to you. What key strategies do you use in your classroom and how does this differ from whole-school expectations? Make a note of the teaching strategies you and your school use in the table below and share it with me on Twitter with the hashtag #MarkPlanTeach.

Strategy	How often I use it

From your initial list above, what would you say are the minimum strategies that every teacher in your school should be able to use to help achieve consistency and enable student progress across your setting?

If you need any inspiration (aside from the ideas I've provided in this book), one place to look is Doug Lemov's *Teach Like a Champion 2.0*. Of the 62 techniques presented in the book, there are some truly stand-out suggestions that could be applied in any classroom setting:

- **'Tracking not watching':** in terms of checking whether a class has understood what is being taught, Lemov suggests teachers be 'intentional about how you scan your classroom' and specific about what you are looking for, despite thousands of distractions. This is easy to put into writing but far harder to master.
- **'Targeted questioning':** similar to my ideas about questioning in Section 3, Idea 5, p. 137, this is about teachers 'asking open-ended questions directed at a strategic sample of the class and executed in a short time period'.
- **'No opting out':** this relates to setting high academic expectations and is a chapter every teacher needs to read. Lemov suggests teachers should tackle the 'I don't know' culture in our schools by ensuring 'all students, especially the reluctant ones, take responsibility for their learning'.

Four ways of doing this are:

- The teacher models the answer and the student repeats it.

- Another student provides the answer and the student who 'doesn't know' repeats it.

- The teacher provides a cue.

- The student asks the teacher questions in order to identify possible solutions.

- **'Ratio':** Lemov describes questions and discussions as a 'process of making sure there's a mental workout in the classroom that belongs to the students' to ensure students do as much of the cognitive work as they can to reduce the work of the teacher.

- **'Classroom culture':** Lemov recommends that we embrace a lesson-plan culture 'that makes errors visible, normal and safe'. Who could argue with that? I have seen this type of practice during lesson observations where teachers are highly reflective practitioners and are constantly tweaking what they do.

If you (or your school leadership team) are able to create a whole-school teaching and learning policy as simple as mine, and can provide a concise list of straightforward strategies to help teachers implement it in every classroom, you will be well on your way to achieving 'collective teacher efficacy', impacting on student learning and making teachers' lives a whole lot easier.

EVIDENCE

In a series of studies published by American Educator on behalf of Barak Rosenshine, Emeritus Professor in the College of Education at the University of Illinois at Urbana-Champaign, Rosenshine shares ten 'research-based principles of instruction' for teachers, identifying the hallmarks of effective teaching that he has discovered in his work over the past four decades. In his research (Rosenshine, 2012), a wide range of teachers were observed to identify the differences between the more effective and the less effective teachers. In this Evidence section, I will elaborate on Rosenshine's findings.

Rosenshine explains that his ten principles come from three sources:

- 'research in cognitive science'

- 'research on the classroom practices of master teachers'

- 'research on cognitive supports to help students learn complex tasks'.

CONTINUES OVER PAGE

The principles are summarised in Rosenshine's report as follows. How many do you recognise in own marking, lesson planning and teaching or in colleagues you admire?

1. Start lessons by reviewing previous learning.

2. 'Present new material in small steps with student practice after each step.'

3. Ask lots of questions and require responses from all students.

4. 'Provide models.'

5. 'Guide student practice.'

6. 'Check for student understanding.'

7. 'Obtain a high success rate.'

8. 'Provide scaffolds for difficult tasks.'

9. 'Require and monitor independent practice.'

10. Conduct weekly and monthly reviews with students.

Elsewhere in his research, Rosenshine elaborates on this list and offers another principle that I think is the most crucial for effective teaching: providing 'systematic feedback and corrections'. Not only is this imperative for students to make progress, but it's also the devil's work if misinterpreted by school inspection frameworks and classroom observers because they are focusing solely on marking in students' books and not much else. More importantly, it's completely pointless if the student doesn't actually act on the feedback. Anyone who has read Section 1 of this book will know what I'm going to say here: not all feedback needs to be written, recorded and evidenced. In some cases, it's often not the best, most reliable or quickest method if you require a student to improve their work in the lesson.

Any teacher who can do all the above – and many of them do – is a teacher I would want to be teaching my child. Even better, if school leaders can create a framework and embed strategies that are based on these principles and can be easily and effectively implemented by all teachers, they will help maximise student progress in every classroom.

Incisive observations

IDEA SNAPSHOT

In every lesson, teachers must check incisively, systematically and effectively that learning has stuck. This enables them to provide their students with feedback and prioritise any particular aspects they may need to explain further or re-teach in the next phase of the lesson. This idea will introduce you to one of the sharpest and most effective ways I have found of doing this: the question matrix.

Far too often, teachers make the assumption that if something has been taught, it will have been learnt. Of course, if a lesson has been planned around the *learning* (see Section 2, Idea 1, p. 61), teachers should be able to gauge whether learning has taken place. But it is not always as easy as that. Learning cannot always be seen. Every teacher has had the experience of writing the same comment in every book or seeing the same mistake in every exam paper because learning was not checked effectively when a specific topic or skill was being taught in the classroom. It is therefore vital that teachers can use teaching techniques confidently and accurately to ascertain whether learning has stuck or not.

You can, of course, ask students directly whether they feel they have grasped the key learning. There are many ways to facilitate this, such as requesting that students indicate their level of understanding with a 'thumbs up' or 'thumbs down', red, amber and green flashcards or hands in the air. Good lesson planning is also essential here; if you have planned your lesson carefully, you will be able to move around the room to monitor progress.

However, the most effective technique I can recommend for ascertaining whether or not learning has stuck is the question matrix. When used well, it allows teachers to test confidently, incisively and systematically whether something has been learnt. The question matrix forms a feedback loop, which is absolutely essential to ensuring that teachers are able to decipher what learning is taking place and that students make strong progress over time.

The question matrix

The question matrix is a tool that will help you use questioning more effectively. It is underpinned by the concept of Socratic questioning, which involves a six-step process of asking questions to:

1. Clarify and assess understanding

2. Challenge assumptions

3. Examine evidence to support arguments

4. Gather viewpoints and perspectives

5. Predict implications and consequences

6. Question the question.

The question matrix will enable you to ask the right questions, frame them with the correct choice of language and ensure the level of challenge is appropriate for your students.

I have taught and observed countless lessons, and I've always found that weaker questions aren't necessarily the *wrong* questions but are poorly framed. Often, questions asked in the wrong way lead to students calling out, closed responses, incorrect answers and surface learning. Examples of poorly framed questions include:

- 'Let me ask you all, what is the…?' (Addressing the whole class might lead to students calling out.)

- 'Can anyone tell me…?' (This gives students the option to volunteer or not.)

- 'What does this do *(holds object up)*?' (Most hands go up in the classroom.)

- 'Would this break if I…?' (A leading question that suggests its own answer.)

It's best not to ask questions in this way, so don't waste your breath!

Instead, use the question matrix to ask your students deeper questions – framed correctly from the outset – to elicit deeper responses from your students. It is useful to prepare your key questions for the class during lesson planning, keeping in mind lesson objectives and success criteria. Of course, you will need to have an effective scheme of work in place first (and I am still always surprised to discover how many teachers consider a PowerPoint presentation to be a scheme of work…). Once you do, the question matrix will help you plan questions with low, medium and high challenge that relate directly to the learning. This will allow you to work forwards, rather than plan backwards, meaning you will be planning questions based on what you want your students to *learn*, instead of coming up with a series of questions for students to *do*, in order to fill time in class.

In many ways, I felt liberated once I had the template for this resource in place, as well as having a long list of possible questions linked to specific schemes of work.

So, without further ado, here is the question matrix:

	Is/does? Present	Has/did/was? Past	Can/if? Possibility	Should? Opinion	Would/could? Probability	Will? Prediction	Might? Imagination
What? Event							
Where? Place							
When? Time							
Which? Choice							
Who? Person							
Why? Reason							
How? Meaning							

NOTE: The level of depth and complexity increases in line with the diagonal arrow running across the table.

I would like to add a word of thanks to geography teacher, John Sayers, for making the question matrix so popular through his blog posts on questioning at www.sayersjohn.blogspot.co.uk.

A few tips for planning questions

When planning questions, every teacher should ask themselves: do I want the students to develop critical thinking skills or deepen their subject knowledge? It can be both. This will determine what type of questions to ask and how to ask them. For example, 'what manufacturing technique are we using here and how does it compare with [another] manufacturing technique?' is a good example of a question that will help develop critical thinking skills. The following question develops knowledge: 'compared to similar techniques used in the cotton industry today, why should this Industrial Revolution technique [tie-dye] be avoided when manufacturing cotton?'

All closed questions, which demand a simple 'yes' or 'no' answer, should be followed up with an additional question. Even simply asking students why they opted for 'yes' or 'no' demands more of a response or an opinion from the student. This could be developed further by asking another student if they agree or disagree with the first student's response and why. You could use the Pose, Pause, Pounce, Bounce technique (see the box on the following page), which supports incisive teaching.

During any discussion, posing a single complex question can often reap the wrong results and confuse or panic students. Instead, try using a sequence of questions to build depth and complexity to tease information out of students after you have taught it. This can be done in class discussions with relative ease, but it is much harder to achieve over a long period of time. Try, for example, to provide and model an answer to help a student develop a response to support improvement.

Pose, Pause, Pounce, Bounce

Many years ago, I discovered Pose, Pause, Pounce, Bounce – a brilliant questioning strategy, inspired by a CPD event led by School Improvement Consultant Pam Fearnley (pamb566@btinternet.com). It is a simple, yet sophisticated, way to tease out the learning in class and support differentiation. It also encourages teachers to take risks and vary their questioning techniques.

Here's how it works:

1. **Pose:** Explain to the class the approach you are about to take and insist that students do not raise their hands to answer the question. Pose a question or series of questions, ensuring you ask the students to remain reflective.

2. **Pause:** This is the hard part. Pause for as long as possible before you ask anyone to answer. Ask the class to think and think again. If students are captivated and engaged, push the boundaries and try holding the silence for a little while longer.

3. **Pounce:** Pounce on one student for an answer. Insist the answer comes from Student A, directly and fast! Of course, plan which student you are going to ask before speaking to the class. Ask Student A to respond and don't move. If possible, don't even speak and nip any comments or noises from the class in the bud. It's magic when you can hear, see and feel a captivated learning audience. We've all experienced it. Wait for an answer but provide support (or call on peers to help) if it's clear no answer is on its way. If Student A does manage to answer…

4. **Bounce:** Immediately ask another student for their opinion of Student A's answer and make sure they explain their reasoning. This can be developed by asking a third student their opinion, irrespective of whether the original answer is correct or not.

In class discussions, it is often best to avoid asking more than one question at a time because students may be unsure which question to answer first. But this is not a rule; you are the teacher in charge of your domain and you know what is best for your students, so don't allow this to limit your ability to stretch your students' capacity to learn, retain information, process and then act.

However you choose to use questioning in your classroom, its impact will be determined by the quality of the questions you are asking. If teachers can plan and compose questions more carefully, they will help increase participation and encourage meaningful learning. So why not give the question matrix a go in your next lesson?

EVIDENCE

There is strong evidence linking the quality of teacher instruction – through questioning to assess learning – to student outcomes. I've witnessed teacher instruction in the thousands of classroom observations I've been lucky enough to be part of throughout my career. In the most successful, teacher instruction is straightforward, clear and delivered with command. Any misconceptions are identified and are either re-taught to the whole class or discussed with individual students, allowing others to carry on with the lesson undistracted.

Classroom teachers who review what has been learnt, modelling and revisiting content to ensure it is learnt securely, are able to actively monitor the progress of individual students. If this is not habitual, students soon become accustomed to plodding along in lessons, as there is no expectation that they might be tested on their knowledge at any time.

Keeping students on their toes in every lesson is key to a successful classroom. If a teacher has the skills required to use questioning and lead learning effectively, this will be a powerful tool that will impact student performance. In her book *Enhancing Professional Practice: A Framework for Teaching,* 2nd edition, Charlotte Danielson writes:

> 'Through supportive and deep questioning, teachers become more skilled in analyzing their own practice. Before long, this way of thinking […] becomes a habit of mind.' (Danielson, 2011)

Questioning is an effective strategy for teaching students how to think creatively, for example when solving problems, and can be used as an intervention during the creative process if a student appears to be going off in the wrong direction. Having spent the best part of my life working in creative subjects, first as a student, then as an adult learner and a teacher, I believe questioning to be an essential classroom tool to develop learning, but mastering it requires a great deal of creativity in aspects of the curriculum. However, 'creativity' is often misunderstood. In 2013, Sir Ken Robinson wrote an open letter to former education secretary Michael Gove entitled 'To encourage creativity, Mr Gove, you must first understand what it is' (Robinson, 2013).

So how can teachers make incisive interventions that support the creative process? Well, as research into cognitive psychology has progressed, so too has our understanding of creativity. It is now seen as more of a reciprocal, fluid and adaptive process. In *Researching Design Learning*, which examines two decades of teaching research and development, Richard Kimbell and Kay Stables look at the approach to designing and making in the Department of Education and Science curriculum of 1987, which acknowledged:

CONTINUES OVER PAGE

'Designing seldom proceeds by way of a series of clearly recognisable stages to a neat solution. There is always the possibility of refinement, of coming at a solution by a better route, or revising the original intention in favour of a simpler or more effective technique.' (DES in: Kimbell and Stables, 2008)

Teachers who teach in creative subjects must reconcile two conflicting possibilities: they could give maximum freedom to students to develop their own ideas and to pursue any approach that seems to them to offer a reasonable outcome, or they could follow a design process that relies on the teacher deciding if the student is ready to move on to the next stage. Ultimately, the teacher must decide what is best for each student, gradually encouraging all students to move towards the first approach, in which every student can develop ideas and solve problems creatively.

So, in a classroom of thirty students, where thirty different outcomes are possible, how does a teacher act incisively so no student moves in the wrong direction? In 'Top 20 Principles from Psychology for PreK-12 Teaching and Learning', the American Psychological Association (APA) identifies twenty principles based on psychological science for effective teaching and learning in primary and secondary settings. The principles include effective use of instruction, assessment and classroom environment, to name a few. According to the APA, asking questions in class not only checks for understanding but 'can help students learn self-regulatory skills […] to enhance attention, organization, self-control, planning and remembering, all of which can greatly facilitate learning' (APA, 2015).

If I were you, I would start planning right now what questions you need to ask the whole class and individual students in each lesson to pre-empt possible issues and guide learning and creativity.

Übermensch

IDEA SNAPSHOT

An effective teacher can change lives, benefit the local community and contribute towards social mobility in their society. But what is an effective teacher? In this idea, I outline seven traits that I think all effective teachers share. Think about which of these traits you already have and which you could adopt in your day-to-day classroom practice to improve the impact of your teaching.

Man and Superman is a four-act drama written by George Bernard Shaw in 1903. Although Man and Superman can be performed as a light comedy of manners, Shaw intended the drama to be something deeper, as suggested by the title, which comes from Friedrich Nietzsche's philosophical ideas about the Übermensch – superman – as a goal for humanity to set for itself.

This notorious quote about teaching has become synonymous with the play: 'Those who can, do. Those who can't, teach.' The quote in its original form, taken from 'Maxims for Revolutionists' in Man and Superman, is: 'He who can, does. He who cannot, teaches.' There have since been many light-hearted variations of this quote, including one extension: 'Those who can't teach, teach teachers!'

As a 'teacher of teachers' – someone who leads on teacher training – I'd like to disagree with this. So, what can we do to make sure we are consistently a *good* teacher, adding value to our students' lives and our local communities? As Geoff Barton says, 'young people appreciate great teachers as much as they ever did, but are more intolerant of mediocre ones' (Barton, 2013).

For years, I have considered the anatomy of what makes a good teacher, or if we think in terms of Nietzsche's Übermensch, what is the model that all teachers should aspire to? Former HMI Sir Michael Wilshaw believes:

'All good teachers share the same goal: to give children and young people the best chance in life. However, the way in which they reach that goal will depend on what works for them and their students.' (Wilshaw, 2012)

So that's the simple answer: a good teacher is one who aims to improve their students' lives in a way that works in their specific context. We know that teachers can have a great impact on disadvantaged students and can change lives. How many other careers do you know that can do that? But how can we make this a reality for every teacher in every school?

Social mobility

When it comes to social mobility, our current school system is failing. The Social Mobility Commission, a government-sponsored body that promotes social mobility in England, suggests government efforts to improve social mobility over the past two decades have failed to deliver sufficient progress in reducing the gap between those from the most advantaged backgrounds in Britain and those from the most disadvantaged backgrounds (Social Mobility Commission, 2017). Teachers work in challenging circumstances, complex situations and under severe time constraints but they can – and do – have a huge impact on the local community. State schools in this country can deliver social mobility, yet current policy means the school system is fragmented and there is little hope of change on the horizon.

The complicated structure of the school system in this country certainly cannot be helping matters either. I've been working in schools for over twenty years and I've come across countless parents, members of the public and even fellow teachers who are confused about the structure of schools in England. We have comprehensive schools, secondary modern, faith schools (voluntary aided), community schools, specialists schools (with a choice of ten specialisms), city technical colleges (CTCs), grant-maintained schools, beacon schools, studio schools, university technical colleges, academies (sponsored or converted), trust schools, free schools, teaching schools, national support schools, state boarding schools, special schools and pupil referral units (PRUs). We even have multi-academy trusts (MATs) and I'm certain I've missed out others. Is it any wonder we are confused? How can we engage, deliberate and decide on what's best for our education system when it's almost impossible to even understand it? The zigzag nature of policymaking has made it impossible to establish effective solutions and besides, the impact teachers and school leaders can have on public policy is limited.

Ed Straw, former adviser to the Labour government on its policy for families and civil service reform, believes there is a better way:

> 'There is an alternative approach to making policy: EDD – Engage, Deliberate, Decide. This means making policy in the open, accessible to all who are interested, gathering and promulgating a real fact base, looking at other countries' systems, and talking about it away from adversarial politics and ideologies. The final decision becomes relatively straightforward. Most significantly, all those involved in making the system work – teachers, parents, pupils, employers, governors, and funders – are committed to it, a precondition for success. With stability, all can put their energies into it operation, rather than into yet another argument.' (Straw, 2016)

For the moment, however, the structure of our school system is something that the everyday classroom teacher or school leader has little power to improve. We must therefore turn our attention to the exceptional individuals (teachers and school leaders) who provide support day in, day out, often in very challenging situations, and make our schools the best that they can be. What traits do they have that we could all learn from to help improve *our* impact on *our* students' lives? As teachers, what form does our *Übermensch* – our aspirational model – take?

Seven traits of effective teachers

Here are seven traits that I think are common to all effective teachers. Think about which of these traits you already have and which you could develop further to improve the impact of your teaching and benefit the lives of even your most disadvantaged students, your local community and, ultimately, social mobility in this country.

1. Passion

Primarily, teachers love teaching and are passionate about their students, their subject and teaching as a whole. An effective teacher is one who is passionate about education, but that doesn't mean they will be on cloud nine all of the time. They are in tune with the classes they teach and the constraints and pressures they are working under. Sometimes, they wear their hearts on their sleeves!

Effective teachers know that teaching children is meant to be a very enjoyable and rewarding career. They accept that students will want to have fun sometimes and they can see how teaching can be fun too! After all, if the teacher isn't enjoying teaching, the students will probably know it. And as Rita Pierson says, 'kids don't learn from people they don't like' (Pierson, 2013). However, effective teachers also know that hard work must be the focus in their learning environment. They know teaching is supposed to be tough. In what other profession would you be given the responsibility of shaping the minds of hundreds and hundreds of young lives?

Nevertheless, in good times and in bad, an effective teacher cannot hide their passion for teaching.

2. Planned and organised

Effective teachers are always organised! So much so, they often memorise the schedules of colleagues and students in order to pre-empt potential problems. Their lesson plans – whether lengthy or concise – are well thought out, so they meet the needs of all students; their books are marked smartly, with workload and school policy in mind; and their classrooms are an engine room. Classroom resources are organised in meticulous fashion, laid out carefully in trays, drawers, cups and pots. You name it; this teacher has it covered! Better still, you'll never catch a student abusing any of their well-thought resources; they wouldn't dare.

3. Reflective and open minded

The most effective teachers know that they are constantly being evaluated by their headteachers, colleagues, parents and even their students. And instead of feeling aggrieved at being held to account, they embrace the challenge of teaching and are open minded when receiving feedback about how they can become even better than they are already. Effective teachers know that nobody is perfect and there is always room for improvement, but they also understand that it is a necessity for teachers to reflect on their teaching to develop their practice even further. After every lesson, they think about what went well and what they could do better next time.

4. Comfortable with taking risks and embracing change

In teaching, lessons don't always go according to plan, so there is a huge need to be flexible and 'go with the flow'. Effective teachers know they must adapt to meet the needs of students and the requirements of curriculum and assessment. They know they need to move with the times; what may have worked two or three years ago may not be so effective today. They believe that they are a subject expert and must be at the forefront of their subject knowledge, skills and pedagogy.

5. Collaborative

Effective teachers have a unique way of bringing positive energy into the classroom every single day. We all have personal challenges inside and outside of the school gates, but effective teachers are able to leave all of this behind the moment they step into the classroom. They do, however, share their worldly experiences with students when applicable to the curriculum. Their positive energy is often infectious and can lift the spirits of their colleagues too. Effective teachers never underestimate the expertise that lies within their school. They never forget the importance of sharing ideas with colleagues through a quick discussion or a short observational walk along the corridors.

6. Able to break down barriers

Of course, most teachers break down barriers daily in their classrooms, but an effective teacher knows that literacy, language and social background are not barriers to learning. They accept no excuses from themselves, their colleagues or their students. Effective teachers know that quality first teaching (see Section 2, Idea 7, p. 91) has the greatest impact on their students' learning. Other interventions are offered but they are never a substitute for low standards in the classroom. Effective teachers set themselves – and their students – high standards and expect them to be met.

7. Consistent

Effective teachers are consistent in all that they do. They may be mavericks but they remain in line with whole-school policy and never undermine their colleagues. With an effective teacher, you know what you are getting (even if they do surprise colleagues and students with unusual ideas from time to time!). Their behaviour never raises an eyebrow because their reputation and evidence of prior successes speak for themselves. They always give 100% in everything they do. They are reliable and do what they do because they love teaching, not because they feel obliged to do it.

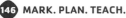

EVIDENCE

In 2014, the Sutton Trust released a report entitled 'What Makes Great Teaching?' (Coe et al., 2014). The report analysed over two hundred pieces of research to ascertain which elements of teaching have the most significant impact on improving attainment. In this Evidence section, I share the highlights of the report; it may serve as a reminder to us all.

In the report, three key questions are asked:

- 'What makes "great teaching"?
- What kinds of frameworks or tools could help us to capture it?
- How could this promote better learning?'

Let's look at how the report answers each of these questions in turn.

'What makes "great teaching"?'

The report defines 'great teaching' as teaching that 'leads to improved student achievement'. The authors identify six key elements of 'great teaching' based on the research analysed. These six elements include the following and are divided into three categories: elements that have 'strong evidence', 'moderate evidence' and 'some evidence' of impact on student outcomes according to the research:

'Strong evidence'	'(Pedagogical) content knowledge'
	'Quality of instruction'
'Moderate evidence'	'Classroom climate'
	'Classroom management'
'Some evidence'	'Teacher beliefs'
	'Professional behaviours'

'What kinds of frameworks or tools could help us to capture [great teaching]?'

The report advises that teacher quality should be assessed using three key methods:

- 'classroom observations by peers, principals or external evaluators'
- '"value-added" models (assessing gains in student achievement)'
- 'student ratings'.

CONTINUES OVER PAGE

The report also identifies three further methods to assess teacher quality, although there is currently limited evidence of their efficacy:

- 'principal (or headteacher) judgement'
- 'teacher self-reports'
- 'analysis of classroom artefacts and teacher portfolios'.

'How could this promote better learning?'

The report suggests that a feedback loop to support teachers' own learning and their professional development could have a sizeable impact on student progress. The authors outline six recommendations for providing feedback on teaching (based on the research they analysed) to ensure 'sustained professional learning':

1. Feedback should focus 'on improving student outcomes'.

2. Feedback should provide 'clear, specific and challenging goals' for the teacher.

3. Feedback should concentrate on the learning, not the person, and the teacher should not be compared with others.

4. Teachers should be encouraged to be 'continual independent learners'.

5. Feedback should be 'mediated by a mentor in an environment of trust and support'.

6. School leaders must promote 'an environment of professional learning and support'.

The report mentions one particular approach to professional development that I have experimented with over the past four or five years: lesson study. This approach originated in Japan but has since been used in the UK and the US. It involves teachers collaborating to research, plan and teach lessons, then observing and analysing lessons to see how their ideas work in practice. It is a gradual collaborative process that is very powerful, yet limited by its time-consuming nature and the lack of time and investment available in our schools. The process is very similar to coaching methods, which zoom in on a particular teacher or student need in order to solve a problem through a supportive set of conversations and observations (see Section 3, Idea 10, p. 160). Sadly, lesson study will never take off nationally until schools have the finances to explore this kind of model for lesson planning and teaching. I can't see this happening in state school education any time soon.

On the move...

IDEA SNAPSHOT

Moving to a new classroom or school can be an unsettling or even stressful experience for some teachers. Here are some tips to help you cope with the upheaval, settle into your new environment and carry on teaching great lessons like nothing ever happened!

Many teachers say that moving to a new classroom or school is the next most stressful thing after an unsavoury incident with a colleague, parent or student. But is this really true?

We could liken moving schools to moving home. Getting used to new colleagues, new students and new ways of working can be daunting. Moving classrooms in order to teach can also be unsettling, I have no doubt. I have first-hand experience and sure, it can be stressful for weeks, perhaps even months for some. Luckily, it's not something I have had to endure since my days as a newly qualified teacher in the nineties. I teach design technology (DT) and by default, DT teachers are used to sharing resources – often with no clue where any of the general consumables are kept – and moving classrooms is part and parcel of any DT curriculum infrastructure. However, I imagine teachers in other subjects don't move classrooms as regularly as we do and for them, it must feel like much more of an upheaval when it does happen.

So, when moving between classrooms or between schools, what can be done to make the moving process as smooth as possible and avoid any negative impact on our teaching or on our students' learning? There are five strategies I would recommend to see you through:

1. Take your time

2. Be flexible

3. Create a moving checklist

4. Pack a moving day survival box

5. Enlist support.

Let's look at each of these in detail...

Take your time

Give yourself plenty of time to move between classrooms or schools. Schools will usually allow you to organise and allocate time to complete and hand over projects. Teachers are very conscientious, so we will have detailed to-do lists that cover all the tasks we must complete and all the necessary resources we need before the move. The process should start as soon as possible to get rid of any junk. It's no surprise to many teachers to discover ten-year-old schemes of work buried under piles of paper in the storeroom! Only take what you need. If you want a stress-free move to another classroom or school, pace yourself and start one or two months earlier than scheduled. Leaving it all until the last minute will only create unwanted stress and in teaching, this is the last thing we want to encourage.

Be flexible

With so many different factors involved when moving from one school or classroom to another (location, resources, fixtures and fittings), things will not always go to plan. You may discover things just won't work in the same way as they did in your previous school or classroom. Sometimes, equipment just won't fit in the new space, even if you've planned your new layout carefully. It's important to be flexible to changes during this time to keep stress levels down. Items such as furniture can be adjusted, installed later or exchanged for something more suitable. It may be worth stockpiling some back-up ideas, resources and classroom strategies (see Section 2, Idea 8, p. 97) to tide you over until you are unpacked, settled and feeling like your teacher-mojo is back in full swing. Often in these situations, it's a waiting game…

Create a moving checklist

Teachers are super organised by nature, so imagine the anxiety levels that some experience when their classrooms are thrown upside down during a move. It pays to be organised, so just like you'd label boxes and hire a few helping hands when moving home, you should do the same when moving classrooms or schools too. Create a moving checklist of what you will need to do and consider the 'other side' of the move; which classes will you be teaching first and at what stage will you need specific resources? Writing a simple checklist will help make sure the process of moving into a new school or classroom environment is smooth, right up to the moment you welcome new students into your domain.

Pack a moving day survival box

Before your moving day, make sure you pack a survival kit of essentials. If you don't, you could find yourself scuppered and scratching your head on your first day in your new school or classroom. Your survival box should contain classroom resources that will get you through the first week unscathed, such as stationery and small storage boxes for essential classroom resources. It is important to have easy access to these items on day one so that you have everything available for your first lesson.

Enlist support

When you are moving school or classroom, it can feel like you are placing all of your worldly goods in the hands of site staff who may (or may not) be available to help you move. But if you are lucky enough to have site staff on hand to assist you, make the most of them. If not, ask trusted colleagues to help instead and offer to return the favour when their turn comes. If you do find an extra pair of hands, inform volunteers of any specific requirements and have the kettle constantly switched on and topped up!

Above all, it is vital to feel rested and to be working on a full stomach when you are moving school or classroom. Ensure everyone involved has a good breakfast at the start of the day. If you are replete, you will be able to relax and get on with the move.

EVIDENCE

If I think back through all of the classrooms I have taught in since 1997 – in art, history, media studies, psychology, computing and in all of the sub-subjects of design technology – every classroom has been equipped differently. Working in challenging state schools, however, I have never had the luxury of using state-of-the-art facilities. Despite this, students still enter the likes of the University of Oxford or Cambridge, or go on to become Olympic athletes and the best in their field. I'm certainly not alone in this. As Jenny Lane says in her article for the Australian Journal of Teacher Education:

'Although provided with computer hardware many teachers do not have a vision of a future world-class education system and are still teaching in exactly the same way they did before.' (Lane, 2012)

CONTINUES OVER PAGE

It never ceases to amaze me how many teachers have worked in the same school for years – sometimes even the same classroom for that matter. Although there is nothing wrong with this, I question why I have worked in countless schools and subjects and how much I might have learnt compared with colleagues who have opted for a more comfortable path.

Many years ago, I made the decision to leave a successful school where I was well respected and successful. Why? Because I was bored. I needed a new challenge and I took the decision to step out of my comfort zone. Looking back over my career to date, I have made some incredibly tough decisions, but as the saying goes, 'the best lessons in life are often the hardest.' But maybe I'm biased.

According to American-Israeli psychologist Daniel Kahneman (winner of the Nobel Prize in Economic Sciences) and cognitive psychologist Amos Tversky, 'prospect theory' is a rational way to conduct calculations that involve risk, seeking to uncover descriptions of the way we actually behave in defiance of supposedly rational behaviour. As with gambling or weighing up the pros and cons of a new job opportunity, known as calculating 'expected utility', we often try to calculate the best outcome and sometimes this involves intuition. Kahneman and Tversky developed 'prospect theory' to describe such intuitions. A key aspect of their theory is that we think about the risks of losing differently from the way we consider the chances of winning.

An important consequence of 'prospect theory' is that you can change how people feel about something by changing whether you describe it as a chance of a loss or a gain. How often has your line manager promoted a 'bad idea' to you in a good light, knowing all too well that you are not comfortable with the idea?

So, the next time you find yourself moving classroom or school, think about why you might be feeling anxious and try to overcome the emotional overload with logical evidence. Consider what you stand to win or lose from moving classroom or school, or taking on a new class or timetable. Rapid reform, lack of funding and increasing workload will be common themes in any education system. What will not be discussed at length in the media, however, is how a teacher achieves incredible results with little or no resources.

If we can learn to equip our teachers with the support they need to work in any school environment, whether they are new in post or more established, (and by support I mean they should be well paid and offered continuous professional development without having to ask for it), our children will all be better for it, and that's something worth shouting about.

The third degree

IDEA SNAPSHOT

Lesson observations should not involve one teacher giving another the third degree. Often, the person who benefits the most from an observation is the observer themselves, not the teacher who is teaching the lesson. All teachers should be given protected time in their timetables to observe lessons taught by their colleagues and to reflect on their own teaching. This is a critical step to improving teaching and learning in every classroom.

It appears that we should never assume that teachers have observational experience. It is highly probable that many teachers have never been given the time to observe a lesson taught by another teacher and certainly not one outside of their department or their school. I was reminded of this only a few months ago (at the time of writing) when a middle leader came to ask me for help with observing lessons.

I am always surprised to speak with teachers who say they have never observed a colleague. If I think back to the time in my career when I was a middle leader, I was always observing colleagues within my department. As a classroom teacher, this happened much less often (but then again, being a newly qualified teacher in the nineties was very different from what it is today). As I've explained already, the nature of design technology departments requires teachers to share rooms and borrow resources frequently. So much so that you are often in and out of each other's classrooms daily, picking up small nuggets of information and best practice along the way. But how often did I have the chance to observe colleagues outside of my department? Or on my own terms and in my own time? The answer: rarely.

When it comes to observations, we should realise that it is not about the observer giving the teacher the third degree. We should understand that observers are often the beneficiaries of observations, as they can learn more than the teacher. Many school leaders fail to acknowledge this, but it is clear that schools that provide time for their teachers to observe and learn from one another – away from any performance management or assessment – have scope to improve practice and impact on learning in every classroom.

When a member of staff asks to observe a colleague, this should not be a difficult request to grant. It is the responsibility of school leadership to make this happen. Admittedly, teachers are very busy and their day-to-day roles and responsibilities leave very little time to observe colleagues' lessons for professional development. However, it is critical to improve the quality of teaching over time and for the professional development of every teacher.

As a deputy headteacher, I worked with other members of the senior leadership team to introduce coaching conversations for every teacher and provide all staff with protected time in their timetables for this. Across the school, this equated to between 30 to 40 periods being set aside for teachers to observe each other and have developmental conversations each week. Over the course of a 38-week academic year, the total cost was around £2,000 per member of staff. It is a substantial investment, but it does reap significant returns for the school, its teachers and its students.

Here is a list of questions for teachers to ask themselves when observing colleagues to help them recognise high-quality practice over time. The questions are adapted from Grim Reaper guidance from 2011.

- Are students consolidating previous learning or learning something new?

- Are all students able to link previous learning with new learning?

- Can students talk about what they are learning, rather than describe what they are doing?

- Is student work consistently of a high standard?

- Do students take responsibility for their own learning?

- Are students able to collaborate with others successfully? Do they ask questions about what they are learning?

- Are students creative and do they use their initiative?

- Do students follow routines and classroom expectations?

Reflection

Alongside observing lessons taught by colleagues, it is also essential for teachers to be given time to reflect on their own practice, considering both its strengths and where it might be improved. Throughout your teacher training, you were probably asked to keep a 'reflections journal'. Is this something you still do as a qualified teacher? It is important that you do, even if it's in the form of an online blog or a series of scribbles in your teacher planner.

If this isn't something you're already doing, here are some questions to help you reflect on your teaching over the past week, term and academic year:

1. What work in your classroom are you most pleased with and why?

2. What hasn't worked? Why?

3. What has been the most humbling moment for you as a teacher?

4. When did you make the wrong decision?

5. When working with colleagues, what are you most proud of?

6. What could have worked better?

7. Who is the one person that supported you through a challenging time?

8. Who have you supported and why?

9. What is the one thing you will keep doing next week/term/year?

10. What is the one aspect of your practice you need to improve?

EVIDENCE

In July 2016 a study by education and youth development 'think and action tank' LKMco suggested that even middle leaders have very little time to observe lessons and support staff development. Only 3% of the 117 middle leaders surveyed said they spent more than four hours per week observing lessons and only 11% said they spent more than four hours per week on staff development and CPD (Baars et al., 2016).

The study did show, however, that being an organised team leader is key for middle leaders to get the best out of colleagues and students. According to the report, heads of department need to establish efficient systems and processes if their departments are to flourish. They should also take a diplomatic and consultative approach to managing their team, whilst never neglecting the importance of managing up. In this Evidence section, I will look at the methodology and the findings of this research in more detail.

CONTINUES OVER PAGE

In their report, LKMco 'identify the behaviours, characteristics, enabling factors and barriers that contribute to or hinder a middle leader's success'. The research was based on detailed analysis of over 200 English secondary school departments and their performance, as well as a series of interviews and case studies, and was broken down into two stages:

1. GCSE attainment data combined with data on the performance of 209 fellows of Teaching Leaders and a survey of 123 fellows and alumni of Teaching Leaders. (Teaching Leaders is a provider of professional development programmes for primary and secondary middle leaders and they funded this report.)

2. Detailed qualitative analysis of data recorded from interviews with 24 teachers, middle leaders and senior leaders across eight schools. This was supplemented by a review of the literature.

The report found the most effective middle leaders to:

- Be rated highly by their line managers 'in terms of their ability to manage a team'.

- Believe that their success is underpinned by 'team competencies' and other 'team-level factors'.

- Believe 'planning and resource management' to be particularly important.

- Be 'open, consultative and collaborative'.

- Have strong skills in 'communication and diplomacy' and 'knowing, developing and building a team'.

- Be 'professionally informed' and able to '[lead] by example'.

For me, this research indicates that effective middle leadership centres on an ability to build and promote an environment based on teamwork, collaboration and sharing best practice. I would argue that one way of doing just that is by using lesson observations not as an opportunity to give teachers the third degree or beat them over the head with a stick, but as a collaborative approach to improving teaching and learning in every classroom.

Invisible collaboration

IDEA SNAPSHOT

Collaborative learning increases student engagement, meaning the knowledge and skills you are teaching are more likely to stick. It also has the benefit of helping to build an inclusive classroom environment, where all students are able to get involved and benefit from the learning activities. This idea will provide you with an effective strategy to embed collaborative learning in your classroom.

Collaborative learning involves students working together in pairs or small groups on a task assigned by the teacher. Students either work together throughout the activity, completing each step collaboratively, or they work individually on different aspects of the task, contributing to a shared overall outcome.

We know collaborative learning is effective because, according to the Education Endowment Foundation (EEF, 2017e), collaborative learning has a 'moderate impact [on student achievement] for a very low cost, based on extensive evidence'. This evidence spans over forty years and includes 'a number of systematic reviews and meta-analyses of research studies'. However, the EEF also finds that in order to have the greatest impact, collaborative learning must involve 'structured approaches with well-designed tasks'.

The EEF also has a number of other recommendations for collaborative learning based on its review and analysis of the research and evidence available. Make sure you consider the following before using collaborative learning in your classroom:

- Students will require 'support and practice to work together'. You should not assume that students will automatically have the skills they need to collaborate effectively.

- Tasks need to be designed specifically for collaborative learning to avoid some students attempting to work independently.

- You can use an element of competition between groups to encourage students to collaborate more effectively, but you should always ensure the focus is on the *learning*, not the competition.

- Lower achieving students 'may contribute less' during collaborative learning, so make sure you encourage them to participate and articulate their thoughts and ideas to the group. (EEF, 2017e)

Back to back

Back to back, or b2b, is a simple and very effective way to engage students in collaborative learning. It is easy to set up activities using b2b in any subject and it can have a positive impact if it is structured in line with the needs and capabilities of your students. You should design your b2b activity with the lesson objectives in mind and you should make sure it is suitable for collaborative learning.

How the b2b technique works in practice is best demonstrated through the following example activity:

1. Sit students back to back in pairs.

2. Display an image at the front of the classroom.

3. Ask one student from the pair to describe the image on display.

4. The students sitting with their backs facing away from the image attempt to draw what is described to them by the students facing the image.

5. Some form of peer-assessment is conducted based on the outcome.

6. The partners then swap over and another image is displayed or the image is adapted (in line with the learning objectives).

Seeing this teaching strategy in action is powerful. Once you try it, the impact on learning is clear. Engagement increases, active listening is heightened and subject content is more likely to stick. It also gets every student in the class involved and listening to one another, creating a more inclusive learning environment. In fact, it reminds me of an orchestra – the conductor (or the teacher) facilitates but the individual musicians must all listen closely to one other, communicating and collaborating in real time for a shared overall outcome. It may be invisible to the untrained eye, but it is effective.

Psychology and...
engagement

The mention of an orchestra and the content of what Ross has written about collaboration both prompt me to think about engagement, leadership and inclusion in education.

Engagement is a slippery concept because we cannot assume that engagement always leads to learning. We cannot assume that a quiet classroom means that all students are contemplative and engaged, and that engagement is leading to learning. Likewise, we cannot assume that a classroom buzzing with noise and interaction means that all students are busy and engaged and that engagement is leading to learning. Learning occurs inside someone's head – it is invisible – and knowing if it is occurring or not can be extremely problematic. A student can be engaged in a task but that does not necessarily mean they are learning – especially if they are doing a more-of-the-same activity where no transferred application of what is currently known is required. Interestingly, being engaged in a manner that is clearly directed towards learning can impact upon relevant psychological factors such as persistence and resilience (Kuh, 2008).

The orchestra is a useful working model for leadership. The conductor has to connect with the orchestra so that they can perform at their best; leaders connect emotionally. The conductor places her or his personal interpretation on a piece of music that an orchestra is performing; leaders shape the reality of their followers. Structurally and visually, a conductor appears to be leading from the front. However, having played in an orchestra, you experience a sense that the conductor is actually leading from the centre. So, as a leader, you can lead from the front or you can lead from the centre…but it is likely to be problematic if you try to lead from the back.

An orchestra is also a useful working model for inclusion in education. Inclusion is a process and not a fixed state. In 2001, I wrote that inclusion is about so much more than the inclusive headcount. I expressed concern that our systems can be far more explosive than they are inclusive – especially in relation to those students, teachers and systems that problematise the notion of inclusion. I insisted that if we are to be truly inclusive, we must move from a tolerance of difference to an acceptance of diversity. The orchestra helps us to conceptualise inclusion in education: it is one diverse community coming together, difference is celebrated, collaboration is critical and everyone's contribution is valued.

– Dr Tim O'Brien

What improves teachers?

IDEA SNAPSHOT

All teachers want to improve their practice, so they can be the best teacher they can be for the students they teach. Schools should support the professional development of all staff, rather than use lesson observations to measure performance and force teachers to show evidence of X, Y or Z in line with an arbitrary checklist, which causes all sorts of problems in terms of teachers' workload and wellbeing. In this idea, I present a strategy that will help schools to develop their teachers, not judge them.

I n one of my all-time favourite books, *The Last Lecture*, Randy Pausch (who died from pancreatic cancer in 2008) writes about his last dying wish. 'The Last Lecture' is a tradition held at Carnegie Mellon University in Pittsburgh, Pennsylvania, where Pausch was a Professor of Computer Science and the book captures Pausch's 'Last Lecture' in written form. Professors who are leaving the university are asked to consider their departure and ponder the things that matter most to them. While they speak, the audience is asked to consider these same questions:

1. What wisdom would we impart to the world if we knew it was our last chance?

2. If we had to vanish tomorrow, what would we want as our legacy?

If you have never read the book or watched Pausch share his legacy in his lecture, it is something I would strongly recommend. The full 90-minute lecture will move and inspire you to take some form of action in your life. It certainly did for me when I first read the book in 2008.

So, if I were to see this final idea of *Mark. Plan. Teach.* as my 'Last Lecture', how would I answer these questions in relation to my time in education to date? What advice would I impart to you and what would be my legacy? Well, the second question is tricky. What do you think *your* legacy would be as an educator? What would your colleagues say about you? I think only your colleagues could answer that question – I don't think you could – so I'm not going to attempt it. My colleagues and the students I have worked with will be able to share what my legacy has been only in relation to the connections I've had with them in classrooms, school corridors and offices. I've had so many micro-conversations with so many of you – some who may even be reading this book or training to be a teacher. Maybe *that* would be a great legacy for the profession. Who knows…?

However, I will answer the first question. Former Prime Minister Benjamin Disraeli once said, 'one secret of success in life is for a man to be ready for his opportunity when it comes'. In my career as a school leader, this quote has become personal. Through the ups and downs – the promotions, opportunities and setbacks – we all need to use our experiences and our learning to be better than we were before. What drives our desire for constant self-improvement? Well, it comes down to the reason we became teachers in the first place. Why are you a teacher? What gets you out of bed in the morning? My answer for you is this: It's the students.

It's not the data or the number-crunching reports and evaluations. It's not mind-numbing meetings and heaving three sets of class books into the back of your car to mark over the weekend. It's not to be told that your lesson wasn't good enough or to be berated because you are one minute late to your break duty spot. It's the students. It's the hope that we may impart a little wisdom on others and help them develop a love for learning. It's also working with colleagues: those who want to help the most vulnerable in society, those who choose to work in challenging schools and be the best they can be for the students to give them and our next generation some hope. We teach because we love learning and we want to inspire our young people to achieve their potential.

If I had one regret, it would be that I have failed to use my wisdom and my position in schools to gather teaching staff together more frequently to talk about teaching, to shape the dialogue and to help them be the best that they can be. If you can forgive me for using such a well-known citation, I will quote Dylan Wiliam:

> 'Every teacher needs to improve, not because they are not good enough but because they can be even better.'

I have unfinished business in education. No matter how many times I've considered quitting and moving on to another job or had to step up to a challenge after a difficult period, I've always remembered that working with students puts us in a very privileged position. As a school leader, I have been able to observe hundreds of colleagues and this has been an incredible form of professional development for me. In many cases, the staff member I was observing helped to make the learning reciprocal. We are all in teaching to make a difference and I would encourage schools to allow all of their teachers to get out of their classrooms and observe each other as often as possible so they can learn from each other (see Section 3, Idea 8, p. 153). This cannot be achieved by only one person or a small group of people observing lessons. We have many, many talented and caring people within our profession, yet observing one another is not feasible or even permitted in some of our schools.

If we do not do something to facilitate a developmental model for school and teacher improvement – one that involves the school and teacher themselves in the process – then I'm afraid I predict that we will never break free from this culture of individual accountability that we have created over the past twenty years in English schools. The retention rate within the sector has been roughly consistent for the past twenty years, but I wonder how many good teachers we are losing to other professions because of accountability and rising mental health issues?

In 2014, the NHS released a report on mental health problems in England. In a survey of 5,000 adults, 26% said they had been diagnosed with at least one mental health issue. The report also found that 'women were more likely than men to report ever having been diagnosed with a mental illness (33% compared with 19%)' (Bridges, 2014). Meanwhile, the DfE reported in 'School Workforce in England: November 2016' that 'almost three out of four school teachers are female and four out of five school employees are female' (DfE, 2017). If we have more female teachers working in our schools, do we not then have a potential problem?

In every school, we must start to address teacher workload and wellbeing. We must move away from the culture of data, teaching to the test and the persistent anxiety of 'Big Brother is watching you' and you will need to show evidence of X, Y and Z. Our external accountability must move to a richer and more formative model for assessing the quality of education in our schools. I don't know what the solution is, but I do know that we are not there yet.

While we are figuring this out at a national level, there is one strategy that I would like to suggest that will genuinely help schools to develop their teachers, rather than simply measure performance and make staff dance along to a checklist. This strategy is coaching.

Coaching

Coaching is something that will make a difference to all teachers, regardless of the stage you are at in your career and the school context in which you work. Sadly, it has taken me over twenty years to embrace this strategy in all its glory because I have worked in an era of education where we, as teachers, have known little about educational research and how students learn. Thankfully, there has been a huge shift in access to journals for teachers; with the rise of social media as a professional development tool, teachers can now organise their own 'unconferences', such as TeachMeets. I am connected to a social network of teachers that I have curated myself and that no school has facilitated. It has relied on my own determination to source new ideas, partnerships and techniques for the classroom and for surviving school leadership. But sadly, social media is not the solution for improving teachers' access to research in terms of what works in the classroom and how students learn. What *will* work is providing teachers with better access to research in every school and college, everywhere. As I write, the Chartered College of Teaching in England is in its first year of development. It is designed to provide the teaching profession with an opportunity to share ideas and knowledge, amplifying best practice across the education sector – from early years through to higher education.

Sharing knowledge and best practice helped me to develop my own ideas of coaching. Coaching has transformed my teaching practice over the past seven or eight years, but my interest in this professional development technique has been heightened even further in the last 18 months. I have been inspired by Doug Lemov's *Teach Like a Champion 2.0*, various coaching programmes and the book *Leverage Leadership* by Paul Bambrick-Santoyo, which have all shifted the focus of classroom observation from assessment to development. I believe this is a mechanism that schools should adopt if they genuinely want to help their teachers be the best that they can be.

This is how I believe coaching could be established in any school setting:

- First of all, banish lesson gradings once and for all. You should never judge the quality of teaching or the teacher in a single lesson, or over time for that matter. Use a wider range of sources to evaluate the collective quality of teaching in a school.

- Stop observing teachers once every 12 weeks. I understand why this policy came about with unions wanting to protect their members from losing their jobs because lesson observations and gradings were – despite the evidence – still high stakes in many schools.

- Instead of all this nonsense, allow every teacher to be coached.

- Identify a group of teachers who wish to be trained to coach their peers and use them to support colleagues. If your school can find the funding to release teachers from timetabled commitments to do this, then the ideal is for every teacher to be involved, both as a coach and as a recipient of coaching.

- As a minimum, coach all staff who are new to the school, including every teacher new to the profession, to help develop 'collective teacher efficacy'. Remember, a school's teaching and learning policy is only as good as every teacher who must use it.

- The process should include no paperwork, only a 'common vernacular' (thank you, Alex Thomas) that should be used in all coaching conversations (see Section 3, Idea 4, p. 131).

Here is an example of a conversation about lesson observation between coach and teacher:

Coach: How could I best observe you to improve your practice? *(This should be the first question asked in all observation settings. The coach should also agree a date and time to provide feedback before the coaching observation takes place to ensure a commitment is made to discuss the lesson on both sides.)*

Teacher: I think I need to improve… *(The teacher identifies **one** target.)*

Coach: OK. This is all I will look at during the observation. *(The coach specifies they will only look **at**, not for, elements relating to the target identified in the lesson.)*

After the observation, the feedback session should follow a praise-question-suggestion-action model:

- **Praise:** The teacher should specify which parts of the lesson they were happy with. It would be even better if the teacher could identify a success or assessment criteria and then the coach teases this out through a series of focused questions.

- **Question and suggestion:** A set number of questions would then probe, identify and plan solutions identified by the teacher.

- **Action:** The final stage of the conversation will lock in any agreed actions on the part of the teacher. The coach should ask the teacher, 'how committed are you to achieving this?'. This technique tends to have surprisingly high success rates. A verbal commitment to oneself ensures the teacher holds themselves to account rather than a line manager or a coach who is there to support the development.

Remember, a 'common vernacular' should be used by coaches in all scripted conversations. Here are some suggestions based on the ideas proposed in this book. What would you add or take away in your setting?

Coaching Common Vernacular		
Mark	**Plan**	**Teach**
Secure overview	Clear and precise	Teachers of literacy and numeracy
Primarily formative	Learn	Learning outcomes
Yellow box	'So why?'	Keywords
Regular	Evidence	Go with the learning
Marking code	Differentiation	Working hard
	Quality first	Key strategies
	Meets the needs of all students and groups	Learning has stuck
	Seating plan	
	No dead time	
	Flying start	

To embed a successful coaching methodology, schools must commit to the following:

- Coaching will replace formal observations.

- Coaches will have one period a week to visit their teacher and every coached observation will last 15 minutes with a focus on one target only. Feedback will take place within 24 hours and be no longer than 30 minutes. The cycle will repeat each week for at least six months of the academic year.

- Every coaching relationship will exist outside of the teacher's subject or age expertise.

- Appraisals and line management relationships will **never** be a factor when pairing teachers up with coaches.

- At the end of the cycle, the programme will be tweaked and the bank of available coaches in the school will be reviewed in line with staff needs for the year ahead.

- No assessment will be made of the teacher, other than a coaching script used to initiate improvements; any serious concerns will follow normal school procedures; appraisal, capability and safeguarding, for example, all fall outside of the remit of a coach and must follow the necessary formal procedures.

I believe if these commitments can be made, coaching will be a powerful tool to improve teaching and learning in every classroom.

EVIDENCE

It is rare for teachers to have an opportunity to observe and learn from each other. And when they do get the chance, they often do not have the structure or language to discuss teaching and learning in any great depth. Why? Because they are seldom asked to observe when 90% of their time is spent actually teaching lessons themselves!

I was delighted when former headteacher Kenny Frederick wanted to conduct research for her doctoral studies at Brunel University London with my school. Her research study aimed to examine what happens when 'Teacher Rounds' were introduced as part of a professional learning programme. This was something I was keen to welcome into my school. Teacher Rounds are a collaborative form of peer observation and continuous professional learning, much like the coaching process I have explained in this idea. However, there are some key differences.

Teacher Rounds occur in the classroom, in real time, and aim to help teachers work in a group to develop their own practice and learn from each other's practice too. It is not a process of evaluation. No judgements are made – ever! The rounds involve everybody in the group, and they take it in turns to be the host teacher, identifying the 'problem of practice' that will be the focus of the observation. The process involves a short pre-round meeting prior to the observation, where the host teacher describes the context of the lesson, talks through the 'problem of practice' and shares the lesson plan. Following the observation, there is a post-round meeting to reflect on what happened during the lesson.

CONTINUES OVER PAGE

The process has its roots in 'doctor rounds', whereby the medical team walk their way around a hospital ward to diagnose patients. If you've ever been unlucky enough to find yourself in hospital, you will have witnessed, possibly unbeknownst to you at the time, this collaborative process taking place among hospital staff. I was in hospital when I was 23 years old, and I mostly saw this happening at 8am after having been woken up every other hour to take medication through the night. I remember trying to stay awake to earwig on what the doctors were saying to one another. What is actually happening on these rounds is not only that you (the patient) are being listened to, but also information is being shared between professionals and this is used to inform the decisions being made.

This is the polar opposite to what we have set up in our schools across the world. Teachers largely work in isolation with their students, yet come together to reflect when no students are actually present. How can our diagnoses of the 'problems of practice' be accurate when often our evaluations are made in hindsight, rather than live in the lesson?

Teacher Rounds are a way to bring an extra pair of eyes and ears to the task in hand (something that we, as teachers, often lack) to observe what students are thinking and doing, what is engaging them and what the resulting impact is. Typically, the process involves a minimum of three and a maximum of seven teachers. This ensures that a range of experiences and multiple perspectives are brought to the process. What ensues is intentional reflection, observation, inquiry and collaboration where all members of the group are reflective partners and can take something away from the lesson.

Teachers who make up the group must be volunteers and must agree strict protocols for working together. When the research period ends, the group can then feed back their reflections and what they have learnt so the whole school community can benefit. The teachers involved will also be in a good position to set up another group in their school and make Teacher Rounds a sustainable form of professional learning.

Psychology and... coaching

When coaching first began, it was a remedial intervention that occurred within a deficit-focused framework. Now, it is seen as a methodology for growth and development. This is particularly highlighted in the prevalence of executive coaching in business. I am an executive coach and have seen first-hand how, in the business world, coaching is framed as being about developing your staff so that you can optimise their performance and potential. In a meta-analysis of research relating to coaching effectiveness, Theeboom et al. (2014) emphasise that coaching adds value. It has a positive impact on self-efficacy, personal wellbeing, goal orientation and performance.

I would like to raise a potential gender-related issue. In organisations, women may encounter gender stereotyping and gender assumptions about ways of being and behaving. 'Executive coaching', as a model, was initially a male-dominated activity. I propose that when coaching women in any organisation, the coach should be sensitive to the particular challenges that women, especially women in leadership positions, may encounter in the workplace that are different to those of their male counterparts. I would also add a vice-versa here.

In terms of psychology, there is a challenge that every coach will encounter: understanding hierarchies of significance. In *Inner Story* (O'Brien, 2015), I describe how we constantly create and recreate hierarchies of significance inside our minds, structuring things in terms of how important they are to us in our world. This is a natural activity, as one way that we make meaning out of our world is by establishing what matters more to us and what matters less. Coaching involves seeing the world from the perspective of another person: being led into their reality in order to help them develop. As a coach, when someone presents you with their 'challenge' or 'problem', it will instantly fit within a hierarchy of significance in your mind. Such hierarchies in your mind have to be flattened because it is how the problem fits into a hierarchy of significance in the other person's mind that really matters.

The relationship between the coach and the coachee is a critical predictor of coaching impact. Therefore, coaching should happen 'alongside'. Coaching is an exploratory and developmental activity and not based on a hierarchical model. Coaching cannot work effectively if a coach is on a status-driven ego trip. As a coach, I can see multiple benefits of coaching at all levels in an education context – from NQT through to headteacher.

– Dr Tim O'Brien

Section 3: Summary

· ·

Teaching *is not* about 'following a lesson plan' to the letter; it is not about 'engaging' students with as many jazzy, practical activities as you can think of; and it is not about keeping students 'under control'. Teaching *is* about helping your students to progress in their learning in a way that works for both you and them, while also ensuring you don't undermine what your colleague is doing next door to you. Teaching is about having a solid lesson plan based on the learning, but being confident enough to deviate from this to help students progress; and teaching is about using marking and assessment to inform where a lesson needs to go next.

In this final section of **Mark. Plan. Teach.**, I have aimed to provide you with a range of teaching strategies that will help you to improve your teaching, so that it can be all of the above – and more! I know for a fact that every teacher in every school wants to be better for their students, but I also know that continuing professional development (CPD) can be a pretty gloomy and frustrating prospect in many schools, where a one-size-fits-all approach is taken and CPD sessions are used to hammer home new national directives or inflexible whole-school policies. As an alternative, I believe that it's important for teachers to take back control of their own CPD. With this autonomy, teachers can determine the type of CPD that works for them and that takes into account the context in which they are working, so it has a deeper and more meaningful focus.

Teachers *must* be given time out of their classrooms to reflect on and improve their practice. Training and high-quality development opportunities should be available to all staff, not just those who are newly qualified, and should be part of our established weekly routines. We all have something new to learn. After all, we are teachers – learning is the true nature of our profession. I also think that schools can engage their staff with well-planned CPD sessions that take into account the context of the school and share evidence-based methods (such as those in this book) to develop whole-school consistency, while also motivating teachers to continue developing their practice and encouraging their creativity to know no bounds.

So, with all this in mind, let's reflect on the ten evidence-based teaching ideas I have suggested in this final section:

1. Be explicit about the learning outcomes and keywords that form the foundations of your lesson through a combination of direct instruction and 'nudge theory'.

2. Apply modelling strategies, such as reciprocal teaching, think-pair-share and I do, we do, you do to help students develop their skills in literacy and numeracy.

3. Have the courage to go with the flow of learning instead of following lesson plans to the letter. This must be supported by a whole-school culture that allows teachers to make mistakes and learn from them.

4. Introduce a simple, evidence-based teaching and learning policy to achieve 'collective teacher efficacy', reduce workload and maximise student progress across your school.

5. Use the question matrix to plan the questions you want to ask your students and how you will frame them in order to check incisively, systematically and effectively that learning has stuck. This will enable you to provide feedback and pinpoint any knowledge and skills you may need to re-teach.

6. Adopt the seven traits of an effective teacher to help improve the impact of your teaching, so you can change lives, benefit the local community and contribute to social mobility.

7. If you are moving to a new classroom or a new school, don't panic! Take your time, stay organised, be flexible, and you'll settle into your new environment and be teaching great lessons again in no time.

8. Improve your teaching by observing colleagues and reflecting on your own practice. School leaders should set aside regular time slots in teachers' timetables to allow for this essential method of professional development.

9. Embed collaborative learning strategies, such as back to back (b2b), into your classroom to increase engagement in your lessons and create an inclusive learning environment.

10. Establish a system of coaching in your school to support the professional development of all staff and improve teaching and learning in every classroom.

And finally

For a generation, teachers have been told how to teach by external watchdogs, politicians and think tanks, by heads of department, senior leaders, and education experts. Teachers have been constantly observed, monitored, judged or graded, and given feedback on what they need to do to improve their practice. Teachers have been made to feel that they are no longer the experts in their own classrooms.

Imagine constantly being told you must be better than you were before. Teachers have come to accept this as their default mode. They have a never-ending to do list and are under relentless pressure for *this* lesson to be better than the last and *this* year's examination results to be stronger than ever before, even if their classes are already meeting or exceeding expectations.

Unfortunately, the guidance teachers receive often comes from those who spend little time in the classroom and who sometimes have little respect for students, teachers and schools. Teachers are constantly being told how to teach. And yes, I must admit, I have been as guilty as others of making assumptions during my 17 years in leadership positions. I now know better and trust good teachers to get on with their jobs. Nevertheless, weaker teachers – and yes, there are some, but thankfully they are in the minority – do make a rod for their own backs when support offered by peers and managers is ignored and relationships with students, parents and colleagues grow increasingly fraught.

There is no doubt that teaching can be incredibly demanding, exhausting and, at times, even demoralising, but we choose teaching because we want to make a difference. We don't come into the job to purchase highlighter pens, staplers and glue sticks, or to plough through non-stop piles of marking. Although it's not acceptable, we also come into the job *expecting* a low salary and longer working hours than most. However, what we *do not* opt in for are performance management targets or reams and reams of data collection that leave us feeling that all our enthusiasm for the classroom has been sucked out of our souls.

We all have our own lives to live outside of school and our personal lives can sometimes influence our career decisions. Equally, there may be factors in our national education system, or in the specific schools in which we work, that can shape our 'love for the job'. But why do some of us grow and flourish as teachers, while others fail to take root? Why do some of us see privilege and inspiration in the role of a teacher, while others just can't seem to find the light in the darkness?

There will always be stacks of books to mark, reports to write and leadership meetings to attend. Of course, we would all rather be picking up our own children from school or relaxing with friends, rather than sitting at our classroom desks marking or nodding off in meetings and twilight sessions. Nonetheless, I believe that we have the power to bring about change. If we make a collective stand against the regimes of data collection, lesson grading, detailed lesson planning and the ideology that written feedback is the best form of assessment, we can change teaching for the better – not just for our students, but for ourselves as a profession. Maybe if we remove the external pressures, we might just be able to make schools a happier place for teachers and students alike *and* improve teaching and learning too:

> 'If we want to improve school performance, we also need to start paying attention to teacher wellbeing.' (Briner and Dewberry, 2007)

I am inspired by Richard Gerver when I say that change is a positive thing. In his book, *Change: Learn to Love It, Learn to Lead It*, Gerver writes about the moment he left teaching and 'first stepped out of school':

> 'You have probably experienced a similar moment, when fear threatens to block your progress. Fear of change is so often the result of imagined consequences rather than reality.' (Gerver, 2013)

Gerver says we should never stop changing and I believe this too. Even though we are reluctant to see changes being made to our education system after every general election, change can be a positive thing when led from the ground up. Of course, we need structures, systems and policies, but not when political decisions start to interfere with the daily work we are doing in our classrooms. We need to strip back the political hogwash and keep teaching straightforward. Teachers should simply be marking, planning and teaching. They should not be concerned with data collection, performance management and (potential) capability just because their last two observations were deemed to be 'less than satisfactory'.

If we do not simplify what teachers need to do and give them the time and the funding they need to do their jobs well, then it will be forever Groundhog Day; issues of teacher retention and recruitment will remain unresolved. We must invest in our public services. We must also change the viewpoint that it is acceptable for teachers to be working in excess of 60 hours per week just to stay on top of their workload. I don't know about you, but I could not have worked any harder during my time as a teacher, and I suspect I am not alone.

We need to strip back this perception that our teachers and our schools can never be good enough and reverse it. The binary methodology used to evaluate the overall effectiveness of schools – particularly when challenging schools are judged on the same criteria as schools in the most affluent areas of the country – must change. A recent investigation by Tes found that no schools in England have had their inspection judgements overturned in the last three years. That's ZERO (Santry, 2017). Tes quotes a response to this from Geoff Barton, General Secretary of the Association of Schools, Colleges and Leaders:

> "'This exposes an ongoing problem with the complaints process. Too many [school leaders] still worry about the inconsistency of inspections and the laborious complexity of the complaints procedure.'"

Having been part of this process almost ten times over, I know that you can complain about the process but not the overall judgement. It's kind of like arguing with a parking attendant when issued with a parking fine. You must ignore the fact that you've been given a ticket and a penalty, and accept that you can only complain about the methodology behind how the ticket was applied. 'Dear Parking Officer, I do not like how you've stuck the sticker on my car window.' Or even better, 'Dear Parking Officer, I know I have parked illegally, but I was not here when you issued the ticket. How do you expect me to explain myself to you when you have made a decision without me even being here?' This is very similar to inspectors having conversations with students without the presence of a teacher. It's not a matter of trust or fear of what is being said; it's a matter of triangulation and consultation.

The same can also be said for many schools that are still assessing individual teachers and their lessons. Imagine a teacher complaining about how they were observed, but not being allowed to comment on the subjective view of an observer. This is an issue that is prevalent in thousands of schools – the appraiser's decision is final, even if they are wrong!

This leaves me with a tarnished view of the schools I have loved working in. Why would any teacher choose to work in a challenging school if it puts their career and personal goals at risk? It makes you feel that no matter how hard you try to better the life chances of the most vulnerable in society, it's never good enough because your successes are still measured by a one-size-fits-all approach. Worse, some teachers are left utterly demoralised by goalposts that are constantly shifting despite school standards improving.

One day, we will all look back and laugh at the current school inspection process in this country and find it unbelievable that it was part and parcel of our education system. It needs rapid reform. I have given my heart and soul to this book and I have tried to distil much of what I have learnt in the schools I have taught in over my career, as well as in the large number of publications I have read. But I ask you, is the book cover an accurate picture of the content? Does the content you have read really give you a comprehensive overview of my lifetime in education? Probably not. I also suspect it may have taken you longer than two days to read this book in its entirety. So, why do we think it is acceptable for school inspectors to assess the quality of education in our schools in less than two days? How do we know that school inspectors are correct in their decisions? There is too much left open to interpretation and this has the potential to damage schools, teachers and our communities. Making valid decisions in school inspections is nigh on impossible. I know I couldn't do it, which is why I refuse to, as would most (if not all) teachers, I suspect…

Professor Robert Coe of Durham University says there is evidence to prove that classroom observation is harder than you think. He shares some startling statistics about the effectiveness and reliability of observers, which further supports the notion that how teachers have been trained to observe one another and make judgements about the quality of teaching is neither reliable nor valid:

> 'A number of research studies have looked at the reliability of classroom observation ratings. For example, the recent Measures of Effective Teaching Project [… suggests] the probability that a second observer would give a different judgement is between 51% and 78%.'

Even more alarmingly, Coe finds evidence that 'if your lesson is judged "Inadequate", there is a 90% chance that a second observer would give a different rating' (Coe, 2014). Our system still chooses to ignore what research says and ploughs on regardless, damaging good teachers and ending careers early. This practice makes it difficult for us to enjoy working within the profession. Our teachers are our schools' greatest assets and we are driving them away!

The statistics speak for themselves. An annual school workforce report by the DfE releases data based on staff working in publicly funded schools in England. The latest report found that 'the number of people entering teaching has decreased by 0.3% to 43,830 (FTE) in 2016'. Digging deeper, the report finds only 74% of those who started teaching in England in 2013 are still in a teaching position three years later. That means over 25% have left even before they've had a chance to master the basics! (DfE, 2017)

A call to arms

Those who have read this far might be surprised to find out that I too have struggled with teaching as a career, several times. As I write, I am coming to the end of my 24th academic year, having started teacher training at the age of 18 and formally qualifying at 23. It's been great, but I've certainly had my moments.

I accept that every profession has its challenges and that there will always be natural wastage, but It should not be the norm that young teachers enter the profession, work like headless chickens and burn out, only to be replaced by the next bunch of recruits every two or three years. Something isn't right about the system if this is considered acceptable. As educators, we all have a responsibility to use our experiences to help change this landscape and eradicate myths so that teachers do not keep getting forced out of the profession.

However, I have reason to be optimistic. Thankfully, there are still thousands of people who do choose a career in education. They aspire to work with children and want to make a difference to each and every one of them. Classrooms are a fascinating place to work. They are detailed, delicate and delightful, full of character, emotion and sound. Teachers learn to love their students – every single one, even the most challenging. Teachers are able to put their 'empathy hats' on, viewing misdemeanours as learning opportunities and understanding that there is no such thing as a bad person, only an affected person. They know there will be challenges. There will be times when the toughest students make teaching impossible. But this doesn't last forever. Children are more than just a number or an exam result. They are our next generation, our next Prime Ministers, our future.

We will all be able to remember a great teacher – someone who has inspired us and helped shape us into the person that we are today. Because of great teachers, children in England are now receiving the best education this country has ever had to offer. Throughout this book, I have shared the work of some of the great teachers and some of the most brilliant teaching I have witnessed within our fantastic state school system. And thanks to social media and the growth of the Internet, all teachers have the opportunity to share best practice and dispel myths created by policymakers, conference attendees and the inspectorate. Collectively, we can challenge government policy and white papers written by politicians who have not stepped foot in a classroom since they were children. We have a voice and we can shape the education landscape. It is our landscape after all, and in the midst of a battering from the media and a deluge of political claptrap, we must take control of our own destiny. Teachers can make change happen. We just need to believe it and organise ourselves effectively, so let's get started right here, right now.

The first thing we must look at is how we define ourselves in the workplace. We all need to be resilient, but that is *not* the single solution for survival in our classrooms. If we do not fix our work-life balance, we will struggle to recruit and retain teachers. Isn't it about time teachers left the school building at 4:30pm? Isn't it about time we had our Sundays back, free from marking and lesson planning? Isn't it about time we could turn our digital devices off so we aren't tied to our emails 24/7?

We don't have to work this way. Nothing is *that* urgent, surely? And no one can drive teaching and learning stuck behind their desk all day. If I had a bucket list of ways to improve teachers' work-life balance, it would include the following. Admittedly, some will never happen, but it's healthy to dream…

- All teachers to have more allocated time to mark and plan lessons during the school day.

- A one-week sabbatical to be offered, accruing for each year of service.

- Any future Secretary of State for Education to be an ex-classroom practitioner. (Imagine that…policies with a degree of understanding!)

- School inspections to be less high stakes and the Grim Reaper's measurement scale to reduce from 'Outstanding', 'Good', 'Requires Improvement' and 'Special Measures' to simply 'Good' and 'Not Yet Good'; better still, government inspections to be disbanded and to move towards a school-to-school process.

What would be on your bucket list?

Staff wellbeing matters. It is not a peripheral issue; it should be a moral imperative for all senior leadership teams and their governing bodies, and this *is* now gradually reaching the radars of those who impart their advice to schools. Although this is welcome news, the day wellbeing becomes a measurable factor in our schools (and that day will come) marks the day that wellbeing starts to have the exact opposite effect to the one intended. There will be sticky-plaster solutions designed to create the illusion that schools are placing wellbeing at the top of their agenda, but 'Cake Fridays' and 'The Annual Staff Quiz' will simply be papering over the cracks. Imagine a swan calmly gliding across the surface of the lake but with feet paddling at an unbelievable rate beneath the surface. That's sticky-plaster wellbeing. It doesn't cut to the heart of the issue; it simply masks the problem

For me, the solution is obvious. The crux of the matter is that every teacher must be able to mark, plan and teach with simplicity and passion. We must give our teachers the space to be able to do these things well and be in front of their students but also to reflect and to meet regularly with colleagues to discuss their students, their lessons and their classroom ideas. That's it. Let's not overcomplicate classroom life with shifting goalposts, fads and preferences dictated by external watchdogs and policymakers. Teaching and learning trumps everything we do in schools and the sooner our politicians, experts and school leaders remember this, the better for our students, our teachers and our profession as a whole.

Let's strip back the nonsense, get back to work and focus on what every teacher across the world needs to do: *Mark. Plan. Teach.*

Bibliography

Allison, S. and Tharby, A. (2015), *Making Every Lesson Count: Six Principles to Support Great Teaching and Learning*. Carmarthen: Crown House Publishing.

American Psychological Association, Coalition for Psychology in Schools and Education (2015), 'Top 20 principles from psychology for preK–12 teaching and learning', available at: www.apa.org/ed/schools/teaching-learning/top-twenty-principles.pdf

Baars, S., Parameshwaran, M., Menzies, L. and Chiong, C. (2016), 'Firing on all cylinders: What makes an effective middle leader?', available at: https://cdn.lkmco.org/wp-content/uploads/2016/07/Firing-on-all-cylinders-What-makes-an-effective-leader.pdf

Bambrick-Santoyo, P. (2012), *Leverage Leadership: A Practical Guide to Building Exceptional Schools*. San Francisco: Jossey Bass.

Barton, G. (2013), 'What makes a good teacher?', *Tes*, available at: https://www.tes.com/news/tes-archive/tes-publication/what-makes-a-good-teacher-0

BBC News (2015), '"Outsource marking" to cut teachers' workload', available at: www.bbc.co.uk/news/education-32513932

Beadle, P. (2010), *How To Teach*. Carmarthen: Crown House Publishing.

Black, P. and Wiliam, D. (2001), 'Inside the black box: raising standards through classroom assessment', available at: https://weaeducation.typepad.co.uk/files/blackbox-1.pdf

Blatchford, R. (2015), 'Thoughts on lesson observations #1: the surgeon and the scalpel', *National Education Trust Blog*, available at: https://nationaleducationtrustblog.wordpress.com/2015/04/19/thoughts-on-lesson-observations-1-the-surgeon-and-the-scalpel/

Bridges, S. (2014), 'Mental health problems', in Health Survey for England 2014. Leeds: Health and Social Care Information Centre, available at: http://healthsurvey.hscic.gov.uk/media/37739/HSE2014-Ch2-Mental-health-problems.pdf

Briner, R. and Dewberry, C. (2007), *Staff Wellbeing is Key to School Success: A Research Study into the Links between Staff Wellbeing and School Performance*. London: Worklife Support.

Brown, P. C., Roediger III, H. L. and McDaniel, M. A. (2014), *Make It Stick: The Science of Successful Learning*. Massachusetts: Harvard University Press.

Cabinet Office and Prime Minister's Office, 10 Downing Street (2017), 'Queen's Speech 2017', available at: www.gov.uk/government/speeches/queens-speech-2017

Christodoulou, D. (2015), 'Assessment knowledge', in J. Simons and N. Porter (eds), 'Knowledge and the curriculum: a collection of essays to accompany E. D. Hirsch's lecture at Policy Exchange'. London: Policy Exchange, available at: https://policyexchange.org.uk/wp-content/uploads/2016/09/knowledge-and-the-curriculum.pdf

Clark, C. and Cunningham, A. (2016). 'Reading Enjoyment, Behaviour and Attitudes in Pupils who use Accelerated Reader.' London: National Literacy Trust.

Clark, C. and Teravainen, A. (2017), 'Celebrating reading for enjoyment: findings from our Annual Literacy Survey 2016'. London: National Literacy Trust.

Classtools (2017), available at: www.classtools.net

Coe, R. (2014), 'Classroom observation: it's harder than you think', *CEM Blog*, available at: http://www.cem.org/blog/414/

Coe, R., Aloisi, C., Higgins, S., Major, L. E. (2014), 'What makes great teaching: review of the underpinning research', The Sutton Trust, available at: www.suttontrust.com/wp-content/uploads/2014/10/What-Makes-Great-Teaching-REPORT.pdf

Cowley, S. (2014), *Getting the Buggers to Behave* (5th edn). London: Bloomsbury.

Creasy, M. (2014), *Unhomework: How to Get the Most Out of Homework, Without Really Setting It*. Carmarthen: Independent Thinking Press.

Crehan, L. (2016), *Cleverlands: The Secrets Behind the Success of the World's Education Superpowers*. London: Unbound.

Csikszentmihalyi, M. (2002), *Flow: The Classic Work on How to Achieve Happiness* (revised edn). Rider: London.

Danielson, C. (2011), *Enhancing Professional Practice: A Framework for Teaching* (2nd edn). Alexandria: Association for Supervision and Curriculum Development.

Department for Education (2011), 'Teachers' Standards', available at: https://www.gov.uk/government/publications/teachers-standards

Department for Education (2014a), 'Statutory policies for schools', available at: www.gov.uk/government/publications/statutory-policies-for-schools

Department for Education (2014b), 'SEND code of practice', available at: www.gov.uk/government/publications/send-code-of-practice-0-to-25

Department for Education (2016), 'Eliminating unnecessary workload around marking', available at: www.gov.uk/government/uploads/system/uploads/attachment_data/file/511256/Eliminating-unnecessary-workload-around-marking.pdf

Department for Education (2017), 'School workforce in England: November 2016', available at: www.gov.uk/government/statistics/school-workforce-in-england-november-2016

Didau, D. (2014), *The Secret of Literacy: Making the Implicit, Explicit*. Carmarthen: Independent Thinking Press.

Dweck, C. (2010), 'Even geniuses work hard'. *Educational Leadership*, 68, 16-20.

Dweck, C. (2014), 'The power of believing that you can improve', *TED*, available at: www.ted.com/talks/carol_dweck_the_power_of_believing_that_you_can_improve/transcript?language=en

Ebbinghaus, H. (1885), *Memory: A Contribution to Experimental Psychology*. New York: Teachers College, Columbia University.

Education Endowment Foundation (2017a), 'Research schools', available at: https://educationendowmentfoundation.org.uk/our-work/research-schools/

Education Endowment Foundation (2017b), 'Spaced learning: the design, feasibility and optimisation of SMART spaces', available at: https://educationendowmentfoundation.org.uk/public/files/Projects/Evaluation_Reports/EEF_Project_Report_SpacedLearning.pdf

Education Endowment Foundation (2017c), 'Feedback', in 'Teaching & Learning Toolkit', available at: https://educationendowmentfoundation.org.uk/resources/teaching-learning-toolkit/feedback/

Education Endowment Foundation (2017d), 'Reading comprehension strategies', in 'Teaching & Learning Toolkit', available at: https://educationendowmentfoundation.org.uk/resources/teaching-learning-toolkit/reading-comprehension-strategies/

Education Endowment Foundation (2017e), 'Collaborative learning', in 'Teaching & Learning Toolkit', available at: https://educationendowmentfoundation.org.uk/resources/teaching-learning-toolkit/collaborative-learning/

Education Support Partnership (2014), 'Three in five education staff are underperforming at work due to mental health problems', available at: www.educationsupportpartnership.org.uk/about-us/press-centre/three-five-education-staff-are-underperforming-work-due-mental-health-problems

Elliott, V., Baird, J.-A., Hopfenbeck, T. N., Ingram, J., Thompson, I., Usher N., Zantout, M., Richardson, J. and Coleman, R. (2016), 'A marked improvement? A review of the evidence on written marking'. London: Education Endowment Foundation, available at: https://educationendowmentfoundation.org.uk/public/files/Publications/EEF_Marking_Review_April_2016.pdf

Enright, J. (2013), 'How do you plan your lessons? #DKL, #script or #5minplan', available at: http://think-forty-two.blogspot.co.uk/2013/03/how-do-you-plan-your-lessons-dkl-script.html

Findlater, S. (2016), *Bloomsbury CPD Library: Marking and Feedback*. London: Bloomsbury.

Flavell, J. H. (1979), 'Metacognition and cognitive monitoring', *American Psychologist*, 34, 906-911.

Gee, R. (2004), *The Usborne Guide to Better English with Internet Links: Grammar, Spelling and Punctuation*. London: Usborne Publishing Ltd.

Gerver, R. (2013), *Change: Learn to Love It, Learn to Lead It*. London: Penguin.

Godin, S. (2012), 'Avoiding the false proxy trap', available at: http://sethgodin.typepad.com/seths_blog/2012/11/avoiding-the-false-proxy-trap.html

Griffith, A. (2012), *Outstanding Teaching: Engaging Learners* (1st edn). Carmarthen: Crown House Publishing.

Hannay, J. (2016), 'How to stop marking taking over your life', *Teachwire*, available at: www.teachwire.net/news/how-to-stop-marking-taking-over-your-life

Hattie, J. (2009), *Visible Learning: A Synthesis of Over 800 Meta-Analyses Relating to Achievement*. Abingdon; New York: Routledge.

Hattie, J. (2012), *Visible Learning for Teachers: Maximizing Impact on Learning*. Abingdon; New York: Routledge.

Hattie, J. (2015), 'The applicability of visible learning to higher education', *Scholarship of Teaching and Learning in Psychology*, 1, 79-91.

Headteachers' Roundtable (2016), 'The alternative green paper: schools that enable all to thrive and flourish', Schoolsweek.

Headteachers' Roundtable (2017), https://headteachersroundtable.wordpress.com

Holmes, E. (2005), *Teacher Well-being*. Abingdon; New York: Routledge.

Humanutopia (2016), www.humanutopia.com

Johnson, S. (2013), 'On the reliability of high-stakes teacher assessment'. *Research Papers in Education*, 28, 91-105.

Kidd, D. (2014), *Teaching: Notes from the Front Line*. Carmarthen: Independent Thinking Press.

Kimbell, R. and Stables, K. (2008), *Researching Design Learning: Issues and Findings from Two Decades of Research and Development*. Dordrecht: Springer.

Ko, J., Sammons, P. and Bakkum, L. (2014), 'Effective teaching'. Reading: Education Development Trust.

Kuh, G. D. (2008), *High Impact Educational Practices: What They Are, Who Has Access to Them and Why They Matter*. Washington: American Association for Colleges & Universities.

Lane J. (2012), 'Developing the vision: preparing teachers to deliver a digital world-class education system', *Australian Journal of Teacher Education*, 37, (4).

Lemov, D. (2015), *Teach Like a Champion 2.0: 62 Techniques That Put Students on the Path to College*. San Francisco: Jossey Bass.

Makedon, A. (1990), 'Is teaching a science or an art?' Paper presented at the Annual Conference of the Midwest Philosophy of Education Society (Chicago, IL, 10th November 1990), available at: http://files.eric.ed.gov/fulltext/ED330683.pdf

Marsh, N. (2010), 'How to make work-life balance work', *TED*, available at: www.ted.com/talks/nigel_marsh_how_to_make_work_life_balance_work

McCarthy, M. (2014), *The Spider Strategy: Six Steps to Outstanding*. London: Bloomsbury.

Mccrea, P. (2015), *Lean Lesson Planning: A Practical Approach to Doing Less and Achieving More in the Classroom*. CreateSpace Independent Publishing Platform.

McGill, R. M. (2015), *Teacher Toolkit: Helping You Survive Your First Five Years*. London: Bloomsbury.

Murphy, R. J. L. (1978), 'Reliability of marking in eight GCE examinations'. *British Journal of Educational Psychology*, 48, 196-200.

Myatt, M. (2016), *High Challenge, Low Threat: How the Best Leaders Find the Balance*. Woodbridge: John Catt Educational Ltd.

NASUWT (2016), 'Austerity driving workplace mental health crisis', available at: www.nasuwt.org.uk/article-listing/austerity-driving-workplace-mental-health-crisis.html

Nazareno, L. (2015), 'From top-down to inside-out: working in a teacher-powered school', in J. Evers (ed), *Flip the System: Changing Education from the Ground Up*. Abingdon; New York: Routledge, pp. 191-202.

Nicol, D. J. and Macfarlane-Dick, D. (2006), 'Formative assessment and self-regulated learning: a model and seven principles of good feedback practice', *Studies in Higher Education*, 31, 199-218.

Norman, D. (1978), 'Notes towards a theory of complex learning' in A. Lesgold, J. Pellegrino and S. Fokkena (eds), *Cognitive Psychology and Instruction*. New York: Plenum.

Nuthall, G. (2007), *The Hidden Lives of Learners*. Wellington: NZCER Press.

O'Brien, T. (2001) *Enabling Inclusion: Blue Skies…Dark Clouds?* London: The Stationery Office.

O'Brien, T. (2015), *Inner Story: Understand Your Mind, Change Your World*. UK: Ideational.

OECD (2014), 'Innovation, governance and reform in education'. Paper presented at the CERI conference (Paris, 3rd November 2014), available at: www.oecd.org/edu/ceri/CERI%20Conference%20Background%20Paper_formatted.pdf

Ofsted (2011), 'The quality of teaching and the use of assessment to support learning'.

Pausch, R. (2008), *The Last Lecture*. New York: Hyperion Books.

Pierson, R. (2013), 'Every kid needs a champion', *TED*, available at: https://www.ted.com/talks/rita_pierson_every_kid_needs_a_champion

Preece-Dawson, R. E. (2011), 'Learning objectives: evaluating the role of WALT and WILF in the primary classroom', unpublished master's thesis.

Price, D. (2013), *Open: How We'll Work, Live and Learn in the Future*. UK: Crux Publishing Ltd.

Quigley, A. (2016), *The Confident Teacher: Developing Successful Habits of Mind, Body and Pedagogy*. Abingdon; New York: Routledge.

Roberts, H. (2012), *Oops! Helping Children Learn Accidently*. Carmarthen: Independent Thinking Press.

Robinson, K. (2013), 'To encourage creativity, Mr Gove, you must first understand what it is', *The Guardian*, available at: www.theguardian.com/commentisfree/2013/may/17/to-encourage-creativity-mr-gove-understand

Robinson, M. (2013), *Trivium 21c: Preparing Young People for the Future with Lessons from the Past*. Carmarthen: Independent Thinking Press.

Rosenshine, B. (2012), 'Principles of instruction: research-based strategies that all teachers should know', *American Educator*, 36, 12-19.

Sahlberg, P. (2014), *Finnish Lessons 2.0: What Can the World Learn from Educational Change in Finland?*. New York: Teachers College Press.

Salles, D. (2016), *The Slightly Awesome Teacher: Using Edu-Research to Get Brilliant Results*. Woodbridge: John Catt Educational Ltd.

Santry, C. (2017), 'Exclusive: the virtually impossible task of overturning an Ofsted verdict', *Tes*, available at: www.tes.com/news/school-news/breaking-news/exclusive-virtually-impossible-task-overturning-ofsted-verdict

Schön, D. (1983), *The Reflective Practitioner: How Professionals Think in Action*. New York: Basic Books.

Sellen, P. (2016), 'Teacher workload and professional development in England's secondary schools: insights from TALIS'. London: Education Policy Institute, available at: http://epi.org.uk/wp-content/uploads/2016/10/TeacherWorkload_EPI.pdf

Sharples, J., Webster, R. and Blatchford, P. (2015), 'Making best use of teaching assistants', London: Education Endowment Foundation, available at: https://educationendowmentfoundation.org.uk/public/files/Publications/Campaigns/TA_Guidance_Report_MakingBestUseOfTeachingAssisstants-Printable.pdf

Sherrington, T. (2017), 'The bell-curve cage: something must break', *Teacherhead*, available at: https://teacherhead.com/2017/03/26/the-bell-curve-cage-something-must-break/

Smith, J. (2010), *The Lazy Teacher's Handbook: How Your Students Learn More When You Teach Less*, (1st edn). Carmarthen: Crown House Publishing.

Social Mobility Commission (2017), 'Time for change. an assessment of government policies on social mobility 1997-2017', available at: www.gov.uk/government/uploads/system/uploads/attachment_data/file/622214/Time_for_Change_report_-_An_assessement_of_government_policies_on_social_mobility_1997-2017.pdf

Straw, E. (2016), 'School for scandal', *Teacher Toolkit*, available at: www.teachertoolkit.co.uk/2016/10/23/school-for-scandal/

Teacher Development Trust (2014), 'Developing great teaching: lessons from the international reviews into effective professional development', available at: http://tdtrust.org/wp-content/uploads/2015/10/DGT-Summary.pdf

Thaler, R. H. and Sunstein, C. R. (2009), *Nudge: Improving Decisions About Health, Wealth and Happiness* (2nd edn). London: Penguin Books Ltd.

Theeboom, T. Beersma, B. and Van Vianen, A. E. (2014), 'Does coaching work? A meta-analysis on the effects of coaching on individual level outcomes in an organisational context'. *Journal of Positive Psychology*, 9, 1-18

Thinking Reading Ltd (2017), Thinking Reading Case Studies, available at: http://www.thinkingreading.net/about/evidence/case-studies---thinking-reading

Wang, L. (2004), 'On teaching inspiration', *Curriculum, Teaching Material and Method*, 3, 32-36.

Weale, S. (2015), 'Four in 10 new teachers quit within a year', *The Guardian*, available at: www.theguardian.com/education/2015/mar/31/four-in-10-new-teachers-quit-within-a-year

Weinstein, Y. and Smith, M. (2016), 'Learn how to study using… spaced practice', *The Learning Scientists*, available at: www.learningscientists.org/blog/2016/7/21-1

Weston, D. (2015), 'Unleashing Greatness in Teachers', *TEDx*, available at: www.youtube.com/watch?v=Ebh7PkuWUe8

Wiggins, K. (2015), 'Teacher's pay rises limited to 1 per cent for four years', *Tes*, available at: www.tes.com/news/school-news/breaking-news/teachers-pay-rises-limited-1-cent-four-years

William, D. (2011), *Embedded Formative Assessment*. Bloomington: Solution Tree Press.

Willingham, D. T. (2010), *Why Don't Students Like School?: A Cognitive Scientist Answers Questions About How the Mind Works and What it Means for the Classroom* (1st edn). San Francisco: Jossey Bass.

Wilshaw, M. (2012), 'What is a good teacher?', available at: www.youtube.com/watch?v=is31rrXubQ0&feature=youtu.be&t=58s

YoungMinds (2017), 'Self-harm', available at: https://youngminds.org.uk/find-help/feelings-and-symptoms/self-harm/

Index